W9-CKH-587

The Rittenhouse Cookbook

The Rittenhouse Cookbook

A YEAR OF SEASONAL HEART-HEALTHY RECIPES
FROM PHILADELPHIA'S FAMOUS HOTEL

JIM COLEMAN

with

Marilyn Cerino, R.D.

and

John Harrisson

Photography by Lois Ellen Frank

Ten Speed Press
Berkeley, California

Copyright © 1997 by The Rittenhouse Hotel
Photography © 1997 by Lois Ellen Frank

All rights reserved. No part of this book may be reproduced in any form, except brief excerpts for the purpose of review, without written permission of the publisher.

Ten Speed Press
P.O. Box 7123
Berkeley, California 94707

Distributed in Canada by Publishers Group West, in New Zealand by Tandem Press, in South Africa by Real Books, in Singapore and Malaysia by Berkeley Books, and in the United Kingdom and Europe by Airlift Books.

Design by Catherine Jacobes

Library of Congress Cataloging-in-Publication Data

Coleman, Jim.
    The Rittenhouse cookbook: a year of seasonal heart-healthy
recipes from Philadelphia's famous hotel / Jim Coleman, with Marilyn
Cerino and John Harrisson: photography by Lois Ellen Frank.
        p.   cm.
    Includes index.
    ISBN 0-89815-864-8 (cloth). --ISBN 0-89815-929-6 (paper)
    1. Cookery--Pennsylvania--Philadelphia.   2. Heart--Diseases--Diet
therapy.   I. Cerino, Marilyn.   II. Harrisson, John.   III. Title.
    TX714.C574   1997
    641.5/6311--dc21   97-15249
                                                        CIP

First printing 1997
Printed in Hong Kong

1 2 3 4 5 6 7 8 9 10 — 00 99 98 97

Contents

Acknowledgments

I am indebted to a number of individuals who helped make this book happen. My special thanks are due to the following people:

David Benton, vice-president and general manager of the Rittenhouse Hotel, for having the foresight to suggest this book and for believing in the shared vision. David has also given me the freedom to enjoy doing what I love most.

Eric Boerner, for being such a creative pastry chef. Without his help, the dessert recipes would not be what they are. I appreciate Eric's wealth of knowledge and especially appreciate his friendship.

Greg Slonaker, a member of the Rittenhouse kitchen staff who worked on the book as if it was his own.

Tom Harkins, for his boundless, nonstop energy and for his great work on the recipes.

Stanley Keenan, for his help with the desserts and for putting up with me even when I gave him assignments at the last minute.

Lori Simon, the "middle woman," for her good-natured tolerance in the face of requests for typed recipes and editorial changes, and for getting the recipes onto the drawing board.

The entire Rittenhouse kitchen staff, for knowing that when "Chef" is not on the kitchen line, he is still working for the hotel.

Madeleine Kamman, my mentor, who made a believer of me when she told me, "You can do whatever you want to do."

John Harrisson, for the late-night dart games in South Philly, for the help with the wording, and for putting this whole project together.

My parents, James and Margaret, for giving me a childhood and upbringing that has enabled me to achieve what I have always wanted.

And last but not least, my wife Candace, daughter Katie, and son Jimmy, with whom I wish I could spend more time. They give me the strength to get things done.

Introduction

THE RITTENHOUSE HOTEL, located on historic Rittenhouse Square in Center City Philadelphia, is a landmark institution with a reputation for both elegance and excellence. The Rittenhouse is proud to be one of just 48 hotels in the country to hold the coveted AAA Five-Diamond Award and to have been named by *International Travel* magazine as one of the top 100 hotels in the world. Since we opened our doors in 1989, we have developed a reputation for the high quality of our food service; our executive chef, Jim Coleman, has been the principal architect helping us earn this reputation.

This book was conceived following the enthusiastic responses from guests whenever Chef Coleman added elegant low-calorie or lowfat dishes to the menu. Some of these dishes proved so popular we would feature them as long as the ingredients were in season, and Jim became particularly interested in the challenge of preparing a year's worth of seaonal heart-healthy dishes. He is a firm believer in using seasonal ingredients whenever possible. Our experience has shown us that people looking for a healthy lifestyle are diligent for a while, but always end up craving the same fare they indulged in prior to the start of the new "healthy" approach. This innovative book transforms those buttery, creamy, rich dishes many of us grew up with into imaginative, heart-healthy recipes, without compromising flavors. Our guests have asked us repeatedly to share our secrets and, since we can never let our guests down, here they are. Our good friend Marilyn Cerino, a nutritionist and registered dietitian at the Benjamin Franklin Center for Health, analyzed and modified recipes, researched the nutritional information, and worked with Jim to be sure the recipes followed the dietary guidelines for fat-and cholesterol-modified diets.

Many of the recipes in this book are favorites from the Rittenhouse menu adapted for the home cook. The recipes prove that healthy food doesn't have to be bland, and it doesn't have to be vegetarian. Enjoy the delicious, memorable recipes in this book. I have been a willing and enthusiastic "guinea pig" for Jim Coleman's creations, and I can assure you they taste as good as they read (and appear in the photographs). We look forward to seeing you at the Rittenhouse Hotel when you are in Philadelphia.

—DAVID G. BENTON, *Vice-President and General Manager, Rittenhouse Hotel*

Eating Well and Eating Healthy

THIS IS *NOT* A DIET BOOK. Consider this an adventure in dining, appropriate for anyone trying to reduce the amount of fat, cholesterol, and sodium in their diet. The recipes are innovative, fresh, and elegant. Sophisticated yet surprisingly simple to prepare, the recipes represent the best of all worlds. They have been devised to minimize total fat, saturated fat, cholesterol, and sodium content while maximizing flavor. Wherever possible, for example, alternative flavorings such as fresh herbs, fresh citrus juice, vinegars, and spices are used instead of salt and shortenings. Lowfat yogurt is used instead of cream. Oil is used sparingly and almost invariably replaces butter.

This book is particularly useful for anyone who has to restrict what they eat for health reasons. Dietary restrictions need no longer seem like a prison sentence.

You'll also find menus for special occasions and holidays to help you stay on track with healthful eating year-round. This book is written in the spirit of enjoying the finer things in life and making healthy food choices increases everyone's quality of life. You don't need to have had heart or health problems to enjoy this book—following a heart-healthy diet is a good form of preventive medicine.

The calorie and nutrient breakdowns were derived from computer analyses as well as on information provided by manufacturers. The nutrients listed are for each serving, unless noted otherwise. The nutrients include grams of fat and saturated fat, milligrams of sodium and cholesterol, and grams of fiber. Calories are reported per serving.

The nutrient and calorie analyses are as accurate as possible and assume that all meats, poultry, and fish are trimmed of visible fat and skin before preparation. When a marinade is used, only the amount of the marinade absorbed or remaining on the surface of the marinated item is considered.

The American Heart Association and the National Cholesterol Education Program offer these recommendations for a heart-healthy diet:

- Total Calories: As needed to maintain or achieve appropriate individual body weight.

- Carbohydrates: 55 percent or more of total calories consumed per day.

- Protein: 15 to 20 percent of total calories consumed per day.

- Fat: Less than 30 percent of total calories consumed per day.

- Saturated Fat: 7 to 10 percent of total calories consumed per day.

- Polyunsaturated Fat: Up to 10 percent of total calories consumed per day.

- Monounsaturated Fat: Up to 15 percent of total calories consumed per day.

- Cholesterol: Less than 300 milligrams per day.

- Sodium: Less than 2,400 milligrams per day.

Some people with two or more risk factors for cardiovascular disease (see page 6) may need to restrict their diets even more. Not all of the recipes in this book will fall neatly into the guidelines outlined here; remember to consider your nutritional intake for each meal within the context of your daily intake. A high-fat item, for example, can be balanced by a lowfat one to produce an average intake within the acceptable range.

The link between diet and health is well known, but medical research continues to emphasize the role of saturated fat and cholesterol in promoting atherosclerosis (including plaque buildup narrowing the arteries) and coronary illness. Here are some surprising statistics:

- Coronary heart disease is the leading cause of death for men and women in the United States, where it accounts for about 500,000 deaths per year. It is also the leading killer in other developed countries.

- Over 40 million people in the United States (or roughly one in six) suffer from diagnosed cardiovascular disease.

- Approximately 8 million Americans have elevated cholesterol levels.

- Every year, over 1.5 million Americans have heart attacks.

- Approximately 60 million Americans have high blood pressure.

- A recent U.S. survey of dietary preferences listed the following items as the most popular: white bread, doughnuts, hamburgers, steak, hot dogs, soft drinks, alcohol, whole milk. Excessive intake of these "foods," most of which are processed and/or are high in sugar, fat, and sodium, is not conducive to a healthy diet.

Low-calorie and low-sodium diets have been proven to lower the risk of heart disease, and healthy eating is also correlated to reduced cancer, diabetes, obesity, and many other health problems. It's time to examine what we're eating and evaluate the changes that need to be made. Our eating habits arise from a lifetime of experiences, family influences, taste preferences, and ideologies. Changing our eating habits to embrace a more healthful lifestyle can take some time.

But it's never too late to begin. Take a positive approach, seek encouragement from family and friends, and get going! Regard these eating changes as permanent. Work on the easiest changes first and then on the harder ones. (Anyone who already has established cardiovascular disease likely needs more rapid and vigorous lifestyle changes.)

Fat: Some Useful Definitions

Fat is a concentrated form of energy and the leading source of calories in food. Fat in foods may be either saturated, polyunsaturated, monounsaturated, or some combination of the three. The chemical makeup of each type is different. Not all fats are harmful; in fact, the modest intake of fat is essential for good health. No more than 30 percent of total daily caloric intake should come from fat (this means a limit of 50 grams fat for 1,500 calories, or 67 grams for 2,000 calories, for example). The current U.S. average is at about 37 percent.

Saturated fat is derived from both animal sources (and especially red meats and dairy products) and plant sources (such as coconuts, palm oil, and cocoa butter). Saturated fats tend to be solid at room temperature, unlike polyunsaturated or monounsaturated fats, which are usually liquid. Eating too much saturated fat leads directly to elevated blood cholesterol levels. It is recommended that no more than 7 to 10 percent of daily fat intake should be in the form of saturated fat.

Polyunsaturated fat (which is unsaturated fat) is found in large amounts in oils, such as corn, safflower, sunflower, sesame, soy, and cottonseed. This fat is healthier than saturated fat and can play an important role in maintaining good health. Consuming polyunsaturated fat in moderation will help reduce your cholesterol level. Your daily intake of polyunsaturated fats should be limited to 10 percent of total calories. Be aware, however, that heat can cause polyunsaturated fats to become partially hydrogenated, or saturated. Hydrogenation also occurs when polyunsaturated fats are processed into margarines or shortening.

Monounsaturated fat, also an unsaturated fat, is found in large amounts in olive, canola (rapeseed), and peanut oils. Like polyunsaturated fat, it can help lower cholesterol if consumed in moderation instead of saturated fats. Monounsaturated fats should account for no more than 15 percent of total daily caloric intake.

Cholesterol is not a fat but a waxy, fat-like substance classified as a lipid. It is an essential substance manufactured by the body and found in all animal cell membranes. Cholesterol helps in the formation of bile acids, body cells, and hormones. We could get along fine without consuming any cholesterol because our body can produce all—or more—than we need. Dietary cholesterol is only found in foods of animal origin.

The risk of developing coronary artery disease is directly related to blood cholesterol levels and the number of risk factors you have (such as obesity, cigarette smoking, sedentary lifestyle, and poor diet). Too much cholesterol in your blood can result in a buildup of cholesterol in the walls of the arteries carrying blood to your heart, resulting in the heart working that much harder to pump blood. Arterial blockage is one of the main causes of heart attacks and strokes.

Unfortunately, when it comes to eating in a heart-healthy manner, many people believe that all they have to do is to lower their cholesterol level by eating low-cholesterol or cholesterol-free foods. However, dietary cholesterol levels and blood cholesterol levels are two different things. While dietary intake of cholesterol does have an effect on your blood cholesterol level, the single most important dietary influence on blood cholesterol levels is the level of saturated fat in the diet. While we only absorb about 40 to 60 percent of the cholesterol we eat, we convert saturated fat into cholesterol very efficiently. Most experts, including the American Heart Association and the National Cholesterol Education Program, recommend that adults consume less than 300 milligrams of cholesterol per day.

It is important to note that dietary studies clearly indicate that you can only change your blood cholesterol levels within your genetic boundaries. It appears that there are very individual differences in how we respond to changes in dietary fat and cholesterol. Some people have elevated cholesterol as a result of a genetic predisposition, but for many people, the major factors for elevated cholesterol levels are obesity, inactivity, and unhealthy diet. However, research has shown that a low-fat vegetarian diet with virtually no cholesterol resulted in the measurable reversal of blocked arteries in 82 percent of the participants in a study. Other evidence also suggests that a low-fat diet along with other significant lifestyle changes (such as increased aerobic activity) can prevent and, in some cases, reverse heart disease.

Guidelines for Healthy Eating

by Marilyn Cerino, R.D.

- Limit your fat intake to around 20 percent, and no more than 30 percent of your daily caloric intake (your body weight will determine your caloric needs). Use small amounts of olive oil when using oil (we recommend buying a small spray bottle from a gourmet food store or plant nursery and filling it with olive oil). Use nonstick pans and lightly spray them with olive oil when needed. Use fat-free mayonnaise, salad dressings, and similar products, but practice moderation. It is questionable whether a diet heavy in fat-free products is healthy. The best solution is to select foods that are naturally low in fat.

- Keep your servings of meat, fish, and poultry to 6 ounces or less per day. Choose the leanest cuts available and opt for the leaner white meat of chicken or turkey. The recommended protein intake is about 15 percent of total daily calories.

- Eat nonfat and lowfat dairy products instead of whole milk products or cream. Milk, yogurt, sour cream, and cream cheese all come in reduced-fat and fat-free varieties. Beware of full-fat cheese especially, which is high in saturated fat and sodium. (Sodium-restricted diets may not allow for the sodium in lowfat cheese.) Likewise, avoid butter, especially salted butter.

- Limit your intake of eggs, as the yolks contain cholesterol. Two or three eggs per week are acceptable, but we recommend using liquid egg substitute or egg whites, which contain no cholesterol.

- Eat at least five servings per day of fruits and vegetables. You'll get antioxidants, vitamins A and C, and other vital nutrients; plus, they are a caloric bargain.

- Eat plenty of fiber. Soluble fiber, which dissolves in water, helps lower cholesterol and keeps the digestive system in good order. Insoluble fiber, which does not dissolve in water, is believed to aid digestion and protect against certain types of cancer. Foods that are particularly good sources of soluble fiber includes legumes (such as beans, lentils, and peas), potato skins, oats, barley, rice bran, corn bran, oat bran, and fruits and vegetables. Recommended levels of fiber intake are 20 to 40 grams per day, or 34 grams per 1,000 calories consumed; about one-quarter of daily fiber intake should be soluble fiber.

- Keep your sodium intake low. The American Heart Association recommends limiting sodium intake to less than 2.4 grams (2,400 milligrams) per day. Foods high in sodium include many canned, frozen, and dried soups, canned vegetables, canned tomato juice, bacon, ham, cheese, salted nuts, pizza, and pickles. MSG (monosodium glutamate) is a hidden source of sodium, and for other possible health reasons, should be avoided. Other food additives such as sodium bicarbonate (a leavening agent), sodium nitrite (used to cure meat), sodium citrate (an acidity controller), and sodium benzoate (a preservative) should also be restricted.

- Your total daily caloric intake should be enough to maintain your body weight, and no more. Watch those calories. If you are overweight, cut back on total calories. The first 10 to 20 pounds you lose will have the greatest effect on your blood sugar, blood pressure, and cholesterol. Set reasonable goals—losing one pound a week represents success.

Eating Healthy When Eating Out

Here are some tips for ordering in restaurants. Many of the same principles apply at home.

BREAKFAST

- Order hot or cold cereals. Choose unsalted, unsweetened cold cereal, such as Shredded Wheat, puffed wheat, or puffed rice. Oatmeal is an excellent source of cholesterol-lowering soluble fiber.

- Request skim or lowfat milk instead of whole milk or cream.

- If you occasionally want eggs, order them poached or boiled. Many restaurants offer egg substitutes or egg white omelets. Remember to request that your omelet be prepared with very little cooking fat.

- Consider ordering fish at breakfast instead of bacon, sausage, or other fatty meats. Or at the very least, order Canadian bacon, which is less fatty (it is, however, high in sodium).

- Order English muffins, bagels, or whole-grain toast instead of muffins, Danishes, or doughnuts. Try eating them plain—after a while you won't miss the butter, margarine, or jelly. At the least, ask for the butter, margarine, or cream cheese on the side and use it sparingly.

- Fresh fruit provides more fiber and vitamins than most breakfast foods. It also takes longer to consume than fruit juice.

- Fresh fruit or citrus juice is preferable to tomato or vegetable juice, which are both high in sodium.

- Remember that French toast and pancakes have eggs in them. If they are served with butter, scrape it off onto a side plate. Maple syrup and applesauce are recommended fat-free toppings.

- Avoid breakfast buffets or all-you-can-eat brunches. They can present irresistible, and often unhealthy, temptations.

LUNCH

- Sandwiches are great lunch options. Choose whole-grain bread, bagels, or pita bread. For fillings, try salad ingredients such as grilled vegetables or portobello mushrooms, or chicken, turkey, or tuna spreads made with fat-free mayonnaise. Ask for mustard or salsa instead of mayonnaise on the bread and use lettuce and tomato for moisture. Limit the amount of meat to 2 to 3 ounces. Avoid cold cuts and cheese, which are high in fat and sodium. If you're buying a sandwich during your workday, keep fat-free dressings on hand to add to a take-out sandwich.

- Skip the potato chips, potato or egg salad, coleslaw, and fries. Pickles should also be avoided if you are on a low-sodium diet.

- Select broth-based soups. Cream soups generally have heavy cream added to them. Better yet, because soups are often high in sodium, order a salad or fresh fruit.

- If you must go to fast-food restaurants, reasonably low-fat choices include bean burritos, tacos, tostadas, grilled chicken sandwiches, and lean roast beef sandwiches. Choose salads, avoiding toppings such as cheese or meat, and use lemon juice, vinegar, or a fat-free dressing.

- If you eat a hamburger, order a small burger without cheese.

- Pizza can be a good choice if you order it without cheese (or at least with only half the cheese) and double up on the vegetables. Ask that it not be prepared with added oil. Avoid meat toppings and anchovies, which are high in sodium.

DINNER

- Pre-dinner cocktails add nothing but calories to your diet (about 90 calories per ounce of liquor). Instead, consider mineral water or club soda with a twist of lime.

- Skip pre-dinner snacks, unless they are raw vegetables.

- Just as for lunch, avoid soups. Good starters include consommé, melon, fish, or salad. Avoid paté, creamed dishes, and fried or sautéed items.

- If the portion size is large, do not feel obliged to finish your meal. Instead, take the food home.

- Request that your vegetables be blanched or steamed and served without butter.

- For the entrée, choose grilled, baked, poached, or steamed fish, poultry, or meats.

- Beware of sauces. Reductions or reduction sauces are usually highly concentrated stocks with added wine, brandy, and/or cream. If in doubt, ask your waiter.

- If poultry is served with the skin on, remove it before eating; most of the fat is contained in a layer beneath and attached to the skin.

- The best bets for starches are a baked potato or rice pilaf. Avoid butter and sour cream with the potato; ask for salsa instead.

- Request that bread and rolls be served with dinner, not before, so you don't fill up on starch and butter or margarine.

- The best choices for desserts are fresh fruit, fruit ices and sorbets, frozen yogurt, and plain angel food cake without icing. Ask about heart-healthy desserts and in any event, use moderation.

Spring

APPETIZERS

Spring White Corn and Potato Soup with Herb Croutons / 12

Chicken and Leek Ravioli with Tomato-Garlic Broth / 14

Smoked Salmon, Red Onion, and Fennel Dumplings with a Curried Yogurt Sauce / 17

Steamed Mussels with a Tarragon and Scallion Broth / 19

SALADS

Charred Red and Green Pepper Salad with Frisée and Garlic Vinaigrette / 20

Arugula and White Bean Salad with Tomato-Coriander Vinaigrette / 23

Boston Lettuce Salad with Braised Fennel and Tomato Dressing / 25

Beefsteak Tomato and Vidalia Onion Napoleons with Balsamic Vinaigrette / 26

ENTRÉES

Linguine with Quick-Braised Broccoli Rabe, Sunchokes and Sundried Tomatoes / 28

Poached Salmon with Braised Artichokes and Plum Tomatoes / 30

Pan-Seared River Trout with Orange and Basil Vinaigrette and Parisian Vegetables / 32

Lemon Thyme–Marinated Broiled Cod Fillet with Radicchio Salsa and Arugula / 34

Pan-Seared Rigatoni with Chicken and Swiss Chard / 36

Chicken and Turkey Sausage Cassoulet with Three-Bean Ragout / 38

Sautéed Lamb Scaloppine with Green Peppercorn Minted Jus / 42

Stir-Fried Pork Loin with Crispy Vegetable Lo Mein / 45

DESSERTS

Thyme and Yogurt Crème Brûlée with Spicy Caramelized Oranges / 47

Three-Melon Dessert Soup with Candied Ginger Sherbet / 50

*Pineapple and Sage Macaroon Tart with Honey-Vinegar Syrup
and Frozen Nutmeg Yogurt / 52*

Tarragon Chilean Cherry Clafouti with Burnt Sugar Parfait and Cabernet Glaze / 54

Opposite: Poached Salmon with Braised Artichokes and Plum Tomatoes, page 30.

Spring White Corn and Potato Soup with Herb Croutons

SERVES: 4

I'm a soup fanatic, and I love corn, so this recipe comes naturally. When I was growing up in Dallas, my father liked the early corn so much he'd drive north through Paris, Texas, across the Red River to Nashoba, Oklahoma, to a large farmers' market where the corn was so sweet and delicious, you could eat it raw, right off the cob! We inevitably bought way too much and would end up having to figure out how to use it all. We always seemed to manage it, though, and one thing my mother used to make was corn soup.

You can substitute yellow corn for the white—just try and make sure it's young, tender, and flavorful. Frozen corn will do, in a pinch. If you like spicy food, add a few drops of Tabasco or your favorite hot sauce.

CROUTONS

¹/₂ tablespoon olive oil

12-inch length of French baguette or Italian-style bread, cut into 4 slices, ¹/₂-inch thick

Pinch of dried basil

Pinch of dried thyme

SOUP:

1¹/₂ large baking potatoes (about 12 ounces each)

2 teaspoons olive oil

1 tablespoon minced garlic

1 stalk celery, sliced

¹/₂ yellow onion, chopped

1 bay leaf

1¹/₂ quarts Low-Sodium Chicken Stock (page 225)

1 cup nonfat milk

Juice of 1 lemon

¹/₂ cup fresh white corn kernels (about 1 ear)

2 scallions, finely sliced, for garnish

Preheat the oven to 350°.

To prepare the croutons, spread the olive oil on one side only of the bread slices, and sprinkle with the basil and thyme. Place the croutons on a baking sheet and bake in the oven for 3 to 5 minutes, until golden brown and crispy. Remove from the oven and set aside to cool.

To prepare the soup, dice all of the potato, reserving the diced half potato for later use. Heat the olive oil in a saucepan. Add the garlic, celery, onion, and bay leaf, and sauté over medium heat for 2 minutes, or until the onions are translucent. Add the stock and the whole diced potato, and cook for 6 to 10 minutes, until the potato is very tender. Remove the bay leaf and discard. Transfer the mixture to a food processor and purée until smooth.

Return to a clean saucepan. Blanch the remaining potato in boiling water for 2 minutes, until just tender. Drain and add to the saucepan, together with the milk, lemon juice, and corn. Simmer over low heat for 2 minutes. Ladle the soup into serving bowls, top with the croutons, and garnish with the scallions.

NUTRITIONAL
INFORMATION PER
SERVING

Total Calories: 213

Total Fat: 5 gm.

Saturated Fat: 1 gm.

Cholesterol: 1 mg.

Sodium: 83 mg.

Fiber Rating: 4 gm.

Chicken and Leek Ravioli with Tomato-Garlic Broth

SERVES: 4

*T*his dish has its origins in the Celtic regions of Britain: the leek is the national emblem of Wales, and in Scotland, leeks, chicken, and potatoes are the main ingredients in the famous cockaleekie soup. Leeks and chicken are a combination of ingredients I strongly associate with spring, and they are complementary because neither one overpowers the other. This healthful, satisfying recipe is ideal for leftover chicken or turkey, and if you prefer to use ready-made fresh pasta sheets, by all means do. Some of the fresh pasta available in stores comes flavored with tomatoes or spinach, which would work well here.

SERVES: 4

FILLING

5 ounces boneless, skinless chicken breast, roasted or poached

1 tablespoon olive oil

1 leek, white part and 1 inch of the green part, cut in half crosswise and then lenghtwise

1 teaspoon minced garlic

1/2 tablespoon minced shallots

1 teaspoon chopped fresh tarragon

1/4 teaspoon salt

Freshly cracked black pepper to taste

RAVIOLI

1 1/4 cups semolina flour

1 cup all-purpose flour

1/4 teaspoon salt

3 egg whites

2 tablespoons water

2 quarts water

EGG WASH

1 egg white, beaten

TOMATO-GARLIC BROTH

1/2 tablespoon tomato paste

1/2 tablespoon minced garlic

1 cup tomato juice

1 cup Low-Sodium Chicken Stock (page 225)

To prepare the ravioli filling, dice the cooked chicken breast and set aside. Heat the olive oil in a large nonstick sauté pan. Sauté the leek, garlic and shallots over medium heat for about 2 minutes, until the leek becomes translucent. Transfer to a mixing bowl and toss with the diced chicken, tarragon, salt, and pepper. Set aside to cool.

To prepare the ravioli, combine the flours and salt in a mixing bowl. Transfer the mixture to a pasta board or wooden surface and make a well in the center. Place the egg whites and water in the well and, using a fork or spatula, fold the flour in from the inner rim of the well. Knead the dough with your hands until it forms a ball. Then, using the palms of your hands, knead for 3 to 5 minutes, until the dough becomes firm, tough, and hard to knead. Place the dough in a bowl and cover with a damp towel. Let rise for at least 30 minutes in a cool place or in the refrigerator.

Flatten the dough out with your hands, and then roll out to a thickness of $^1/_{16}$ inch or less (if using a pasta machine, use a setting of 3). Using a 4-inch round cutter, cut out 12 circles of pasta. Brush the egg wash in a $^1/_2$-inch strip along the edge of each pasta round. Place 1 tablespoon of the reserved filling on each round and fold over in a half-moon shape. Gently seal the edges together with your fingers, removing all the air from each ravioli.

To prepare the broth, place the tomato paste in a sauté pan and stir constantly over medium heat for 2 minutes. Stir in the garlic, tomato juice, and stock, and reduce by one-quarter. Keep warm.

Bring the water to a boil in a saucepan. Slice the remaining half of the leek lengthwise and blanch in the boiling water for 2 minutes. Remove with a slotted spoon, refresh under cold running water, and set aside. Place the ravioli in the boiling water and boil for 5 minutes, or until al dente. Drain. Ladle about $^1/_3$ cup of the broth into each serving bowl. Arrange 3 ravioli on top of the broth and garnish with the blanched leeks.

NUTRITIONAL
INFORMATION PER
SERVING

Total Calories: 375

Total Fat: 5 gm.

Saturated Fat: 1 gm.

Cholesterol: 38 mg.

Sodium: 577 mg.

Fiber Rating: 3 gm.

Smoked Salmon, Red Onion, and Fennel Dumplings with Curried Yogurt Sauce

SERVES: 4

These dumplings are inspired by street food I tasted while I was visiting China in 1990. It was around the time of the Tiananmen Square disturbances, and we had to leave the country after martial law was introduced. While I was in Beijing, I loved trying different foods sold by street vendors— every trip I take abroad revolves around food! Fennel, salmon, and red onion make a natural marriage of taste. Fennel is available through the winter and spring, and its fragrant, sweet, and delicate anise-like flavor works wonderfully well with salmon. In turn, the rich salmon and the aromatic fennel are smoothed out by the curried yogurt sauce. Don't be intimidated by the curry, which is pleasantly mild, proving that curry does not have to be hot to be effective.

FILLING

2 teaspoons olive oil

1 red onion, finely diced

1 fennel bulb, finely diced

$1/4$ teaspoon minced garlic

$1/4$ teaspoon minced shallots

2 ounces smoked salmon, finely diced

1 teaspoon minced fresh basil

12 round wonton wrappers

1 head frisée lettuce (or curly endive)

SAUCE

$1/3$ cup Low-Sodium Chicken Stock (page 225)

2 teaspoons curry powder

$1/2$ cup nonfat yogurt

1 tablespoon chopped fresh dill

NUTRITIONAL
INFORMATION PER
SERVING

Total Calories: 143

Total Fat: 3 gm.

Saturated Fat: 1 gm.

Cholesterol: 61 mg.

Sodium: 205 mg.

Fiber Rating: 2 gm

To prepare the filling, heat the olive oil in a sauté pan. Add the onion, fennel, garlic, and shallot to the hot pan, and sauté over medium-high heat for 2 to 3 minutes, until tender. Remove the pan from the heat and let cool slightly. Stir in the salmon and basil and set aside.

To prepare the sauce, whisk together the chicken stock and curry powder in a small saucepan, and bring to a boil over high heat. Remove the pan from the heat and let cool slightly. Stir in the yogurt and dill and set aside to cool completely.

Brush the edges of the wonton wrappers with a little water. Place 1 table-spoon of the filling in the center of each wrapper and fold the sides over to create half-moons. Firmly seal the edges with your fingers, removing all the air from the dumplings. (If you are using square wonton wrappers, fold the opposite edges together to form triangles.)

Bring 2 quarts of water to a boil in a saucepan. Carefully drop the dumplings into the boiling water and poach for about 3 minutes, until soft. Remove with a slotted spoon and drain on paper towels. Coat a sauté pan with nonstick cooking spray and place over high heat. Add the dumplings to the hot pan and quickly sauté for 1 to $1^1/_2$ minutes on each side, until brown.

With a small pastry brush, paint the plate in an artistic pattern with the yogurt and place a small amount of frisée at the top of the plate (in the 12 o'clock position). Place the dumplings shingle-style, so they overlap each other, down the center of the plate and serve.

Steamed Mussels with a Tarragon and Scallion Broth

elieve it or not, my daughter Katie, 11, is a mussel fanatic, and this recipe is dedicated to her. On her first day of kindergarten, her classmates were asked to name their favorite foods. A consensus was building—MacDonald's, pizza, peanut butter, hot dogs—when Katie let loose with "mussels and sushi." Ah, the perils of being a chef's daughter! Her teacher was understandably speechless. Katie may not eat much, and she may be picky, but she can just about eat her weight in mussels. Mussels are a spring-season shellfish in California, but are generally available year-round. Tarragon is an assertively flavored herb with subtly aromatic tones; a little goes a long way.

SERVES: 4

24 black mussels, debearded and washed

2 cups white wine

1 cup clam juice

2 tablespoons minced garlic

2 teaspoons minced shallots, white and green parts separate

4 scallions, white parts sliced lengthwise, and green parts sliced crosswise

2 large tomatoes, peeled, seeded, and chopped

2 bay leaves

2 tablespoons chopped fresh tarragon

Juice of 1 lemon

NUTRITIONAL INFORMATION PER SERVING

Total Calories: 169

Total Fat: 2 gm.

Saturated Fat: 0 gm.

Cholesterol: 40 mg.

Sodium: 411 mg.

Fiber Rating: 1 gm.

Place the mussels, wine, clam juice, garlic, shallots, white parts of the scallions, tomatoes, and bay leaves in a large skillet or heavy-bottomed saucepan. Cover the skillet and bring the mixture to a simmer over high heat. Simmer for about 5 minutes, or until the mussels have fully opened. Discard any mussels that remain closed. Add the green parts of the scallions, the tarragon, and lemon juice.

Arrange 6 mussels in each serving bowl. Using a slotted spoon, arrange the tomatoes and scallions in the center of the bowls. Add the broth and serve.

Charred Red and Green Pepper Salad with Frisée and Garlic Vinaigrette

SERVES: 4

This is a fun, easy recipe, and the colors make a striking presentation. If you can find yellow or orange peppers, use them, too. (Purple and chocolate peppers are nice, but they are a little harder to come by.) Another means of enhancing the presentation of this salad is to mound the lettuce to give the dish extra height. Frisée is a member of the escarole family, and has a crunchy texture and an intriguing, slightly peppery, bitter flavor. You can substitute a combination of Belgian endive and romaine lettuce, if you prefer.

PEPPERS

3 red bell peppers

$^1/_2$ teaspoon olive oil

1 green bell pepper, seeded and sliced lengthwise into $^1/_2$-inch strips

VINAIGRETTE

4 teaspoons olive oil

$^1/_2$ teaspoon minced garlic

2 tablespoons balsamic vinegar

SALAD

2 heads frisée lettuce

Freshly cracked black pepper to taste

8 to 12 chives, for garnish

Coat 2 of the red bell peppers with $^1/_4$ teaspoon of the olive oil. Roast, peel, cut in half, and remove the seeds and internal ribs (see page 231). Set aside.

Preheat the broiler to high. Cut the remaining red bell peppers in half, remove the seeds, and slice lengthwise into $^1/_2$-inch strips. Place in a mixing bowl and toss with the remaining $^1/_4$ teaspoon of olive oil. Arrange the bell peppers on a baking sheet and place under the broiler, until they begin to turn brown. Turn the bell peppers over and continue cooking until charred (mostly brown with black streaks, and not yet roasted). Set aside to cool. (Charring the peppers gives them an interesting roasted flavor, and it's a healthy way to cook them; however, if you find it easier, you can sauté them in a skillet.)

To prepare the vinaigrette, heat the olive oil in a sauté pan. Add the garlic to the hot pan and sauté over medium-high heat for 2 to 3 minutes, until golden brown. Transfer to a mixing bowl and whisk in the balsamic vinegar. Set aside to cool.

Place one flattened half of a roasted red bell pepper at the top of each plate (at the 12 o'clock position). Mound the frisée in the center of the plate and sprinkle the black pepper around it. Stack the green bell peppers at the bottom of the plate (at the 6 o'clock position), alternating the colors. Drizzle a little of the vinaigrette on either side of the frisée; garnish the frisée with the chives.

NUTRITIONAL
INFORMATION PER
SERVING

Total Calories: 77

Total Fat: 5 gm.

Saturated Fat: 1 gm.

Cholesterol: 0 mg.

Sodium: 5 mg.

Fiber Rating: 2 gm.

Arugula and White Bean Salad with Tomato-Coriander Vinaigrette

This simple salad is inspired by a traditional spring dish I enjoyed in Portugal, where the salad was accompanied by bacalao (salt cod) cakes. Here, the peppery arugula is balanced by the rich white beans, and the Mediterranean-flavored vinaigrette brings both ingredients together. In Portugal, they use the smaller white navy beans, so use those, or use the larger white Northern beans.

SERVES: 6

BEANS

12 ounces dried white navy beans, rinsed and soaked overnight

VINAIGRETTE

1 large tomato, blanched, peeled, cut in half, seeded, and coarsely chopped (about 1 cup)

$^1/_2$ cup white wine vinegar

1 tablespoon coriander seeds

4 teaspoons canola oil

Freshly cracked black pepper to taste

SALAD

6 ounces arugula

2 small tomatoes, blanched, peeled, seeded, and diced

6 tablespoons julienned fresh basil

Drain and rinse the beans and place in a large saucepan. Add enough cold water to cover the beans by $^1/_2$ inch. Bring the beans to a boil over high heat. Reduce the heat to a simmer and cook the beans for about 1 to $1^1/_2$ hours, until tender. Add more water if necessary to keep the beans covered. Drain the beans and let cool.

NUTRITIONAL
INFORMATION PER
SERVING

Total Calories: 243

Total Fat: 6 gm.

Saturated Fat: 1 gm.

Cholesterol: 0 mg.

Sodium: 23 mg.

Fiber Rating: 1 gm.

To prepare the vinaigrette, place the tomatoes, vinegar, and coriander in a saucepan. Bring to a boil over medium-high heat and reduce by one-half. Remove from the heat and let cool. Add the canola oil and pepper, transfer to a blender, and purée until smooth. Place the cooked beans in a mixing bowl and toss with $^1/_2$ cup of the vinaigrette.

To prepare the salad, place a steamer basket over a saucepan of boiling water. Place the arugula in the steamer basket and steam for 1 to 1 $^1/_2$ minutes, until wilted. Place the arugula in a separate mixing bowl, and toss with $^1/_4$ cup of the vinaigrette.

Arrange the tossed arugula in a strip running down the center of each serving plate. Place the beans at the bottom of each plate, slightly overlapping the arugula. Place the tomatoes and basil over the arugula, and serve the remaining vinaigrette on the side.

NOTE: Most of the calories in this recipe are from the canola oil; however, it's a "good" oil in that it is lower in saturated fat than any other oil and has higher levels of monounsaturated fat than all other oils, except olive oil.

Boston Lettuce Salad with Braised Fennel and Tomato Dressing

oston lettuce and fennel are two ingredients that once seemed exotic, but are now often seen on the dinner table. This simple, mild-flavored spring salad makes a great introduction to any meal with bold, assertive flavors.

SERVES: 4

DRESSING

$1/3$ cup red wine vinegar

1 teaspoon minced garlic

$1/4$ teaspoon minced shallots

1 teaspoon sugar

4 teaspoons olive oil

3 tablespoons Low-Sodium Chicken Stock (page 225)

1 large fennel bulb, cored and julienned

1 large tomato, blanched, peeled, seeded, and julienned

SALAD

2 heads Boston or Bibb lettuce, cut in half

2 tablespoons sliced fresh chives, for garnish

NUTRITIONAL INFORMATION PER SERVING

Total Calories: 76

Total Fat: 5 gm.

Saturated Fat: 1 gm.

Cholesterol: 0

Sodium: 78 mg.

Fiber Rating: 3 gm.

To prepare the dressing, thoroughly whisk together the vinegar, garlic, shallot, and sugar in a mixing bowl. Let sit for 2 to 3 minutes, then slowly whisk in the olive oil and chicken stock. Set aside.

Bring a saucepan of water to a boil. Add the fennel and blanch for 4 minutes. Drain the fennel, transfer to a saucepan, and add the julienned tomato and the reserved dressing. Bring to a simmer over medium-high heat and immediately remove from the heat.

Place half a head of lettuce on each serving plate and drizzle with the warm vinaigrette. Garnish with the chives and serve.

Beefsteak Tomato and Vidalia Onion Napoleons with Balsamic Vinaigrette

SERVES: 4

This is a fun way to serve beefsteak tomatoes, and it's also a great showcase for sweet onions. My parents' relatives, who live in Georgia, used to send us packages of the deliciously sweet Vidalia onions when I was growing up. (This was in the days before the 10/15 variety of sweet onion— later known as the Texas Noon Day, which was developed at Texas A&M University.) My mother would make salads by mixing the Vidalias with farm stand tomatoes; this recipe is an upgraded version of that childhood fare. Use Walla Walla sweet onions from Washington State or Maui onions if the Vidalia or Texas Noon Day varieties are unavailable in your area. Sweet onions have a higher water content than regular onions, and are therefore more perishable, so be sure to use them soon after purchase. Unlike the basil, which is a classic partner with tomatoes, the addition of mint may seem a little unusual, but it works very well with the sweetness of the onion and complements the basil and tomatoes nicely.

BALSAMIC VINAIGRETTE

2 tablespoons balsamic vinegar

4 tablespoons olive oil

1 tablespoon minced garlic

1 teaspoon sugar

$^1/_4$ teaspoon salt

NAPOLEONS

3 large (beefsteak) tomatoes, preferably vine-ripened, cut into 4 slices each (about $^1/_2$ inch thick)

1 large Vidalia, Texas Noon Day, Maui, or other sweet onion, cut into 8 slices

16 fresh basil leaves

16 fresh mint leaves

Freshly ground black pepper to taste

Thoroughly whisk together all of the vinaigrette ingredients in a mixing bowl and set aside.

To prepare the salad, place 4 slices of the tomato on a work surface and top each with 1 slice of the onion. Place 2 basil leaves and 2 mint leaves on top of each onion layer and sprinkle with the pepper. Place 1 tomato slice on top of the mint and basil, and then repeat with layers of the onion, basil, mint, and pepper. Place a final slice of tomato on top of each napoleon, and skewer with 2 toothpicks each (one towards each end) to hold them together.

Slice each napoleon in half and arrange on a serving plate in a "V" shape so that it opens to show the interior layers. Remove the toothpicks and drizzle each napoleon with 1 tablespoon of the vinaigrette.

NOTE: The salt in this recipe is needed to bring out the full flavor of the tomatoes, while the sugar cuts the acidity of the vinaigrette; however, you can reduce the amounts if you like. The fat in this recipe is largely LDL-lowering monounsaturated fat found in the olive oil. To lower the fat content, use less vinaigrette.

NUTRITIONAL INFORMATION PER SERVING

Total Calories: 137

Total Fat: 8 gm.

Saturated Fat: 1 gm.

Cholesterol: 0 mg.

Sodium: 104 mg.

Fiber Rating: 4 gm.

Linguine with Quick-Braised Broccoli Rabe, Sunchokes and Sun-Dried Tomatoes

SERVES: 4

Broccoli rabe (or raab), also called choy sum in Chinese markets and rapini in Italian markets, is a type of broccoli related to turnips. It does not produce the large florets of cauliflowers, although it does grow small clusters of miniature buds. Broccoli rabe has a pungently tart but attractively intense flavor that is counterbalanced beautifully by the rich Jerusalem artichokes, commonly called sunchokes. These are tubers, native to North America, are members of the sunflower family; they are not related to artichokes. Neither do they have any connection with Jerusalem; the name is most likely a corruption of the Italian name "girasole," by which they were originally marketed, or beccause early colonial settlers associated the taste with the more familiar artichoke. This is a great vegetarian spring dish—light, refreshing, and full of flavor.

PASTA

1 pound dried linguine

SAUCE

1 tablespoon olive oil

2 tablespoons minced garlic

8 ounces sunchokes (Jerusalem artichokes), peeled and thinly sliced

8 ounces broccoli rabe

$^3/_4$ cup dry-packed sundried tomatoes, rehydrated and julienned

1 cup white wine

2 cups Low-Sodium Chicken Stock (page 225)

1 tablespoon freshly squeezed lemon juice

2 tablespoons balsamic vinegar

$^1/_4$ cup chopped fresh basil

$^1/_2$ teaspoon salt

Freshly cracked black pepper to taste

4 sprigs basil, for garnish

To prepare the pasta, bring a saucepan of salted water to a boil. Add the linguine, return to a boil, and cook for 8 to 12 minutes, until al dente. Drain and let cool.

To prepare the sauce, heat the olive oil in a large nonstick sauté pan. Add the garlic, sunchokes, broccoli rabe, and sundried tomatoes, and sauté for 2 minutes over medium-high heat, stirring frequently. Deglaze with the wine and reduce by three-quarters. Add the chicken stock and reduce by one-half. Stir in the lemon juice, vinegar, chopped basil, salt, and pepper and cook for 1 minute longer.

Add the reserved linguine and toss to coat thoroughly. Divide the pasta between serving bowls and garnish with the basil sprigs.

❧

NOTE: The vegetables, and especially the broccoli rabe, provide the high fiber in this dish. To significantly reduce the number of calories, serve with only 8 to 10 ounces of linguine.

NUTRITIONAL
INFORMATION PER
SERVING

Total Calories: 583

Total Fat: 6 gm.

Saturated Fat: 1 gm.

Cholesterol: 0 mg.

Sodium: 331 mg.

Fiber Rating: 9 gm.

Poached Salmon with Braised Artichokes and Plum Tomatoes

SERVES: 4

*W*hen the first salmon runs begin in May, my thoughts turn to preparing this noble fish. The best salmon I ever tasted, not surprisingly, was in Alaska; my father and I are both keen anglers, and we'd fillet and grill the marvelous Copper River salmon we caught right away—there's nothing quite like it. Artichokes make excellent partners for salmon. Their mild flavors go well together, and they both have a pleasant "mouth-feel." Using frozen artichokes will save you a lot of time, but use fresh artichokes if you can. Avoid the canned variety, which are high in sodium and are not as flavorful. Salmon and dill is another pairing that married a while ago and a divorce is not likely any time soon! If you're ever in doubt about which flavors to match with salmon, you can never go wrong with dill. This is an attractive entrée, especially when presented in a large serving bowl. This dish can be served with Radicchio Salsa (page 34).

1 cup white wine

1 cup salt-free clam juice

$^1/_3$ cup water

1 tablespoon balsamic vinegar

1 teaspoon chopped garlic

1 tablespoon chopped shallots

4 large plum tomatoes, blanched, peeled, seeded, and diced

7 ounces frozen artichoke bottoms, washed and diced (or fresh artichoke bottoms, cooked)

4 boneless, skinless salmon fillets, about 5 ounces each

Juice of 1 lemon

1 tablespoon chopped fresh dill

GARNISH:

4 dill sprigs

4 lemon slices

Place the wine, clam juice, water, vinegar, garlic, shallots, tomatoes, and artichoke bottoms in a saucepan. Carefully place the salmon fillets on top of the ingredients in the pan. Bring to a simmer, reduce the heat to medium, and poach for about 10 minutes, until cooked medium-rare to medium. (The salmon is cooked medium-well to well-done if the white albumen rises to the surface.) Remove the salmon and keep warm.

Stir the lemon juice and chopped dill into the poaching liquid. Divide the sauce between serving bowls and top with the salmon fillets. Garnish with the dill sprigs and lemon slices, and serve.

❧

NOTE: The sodium content of this low-calorie dish will be much increased if you use a sodium-based clam juice or canned artichokes.

NUTRITIONAL INFORMATION PER SERVING

Total Calories: 340

Total Fat: 9 gm.

Saturated Fat: 2 gm.

Cholesterol: 70 mg.

Sodium: 150 mg.

Fiber Rating: 2 gm.

Pan-Seared River Trout with Orange and Basil Vinaigrette and Parisian Vegetables

SERVES: 4

Trout fishing was a pastime I always looked forward to when I was growing up in Texas. My family had a weekend and holiday home in the Oklahoma mountains close to the Arkansas border. Brown river trout were plentiful in the cool mountain streams during the spring months; later on, in the warmer summer weather, bass were the predominant sport fish. Pennsylvania also has abundant trout streams, but thanks to the growing popularity of fish farming in recent years, trout are now available year-round. At the Rittenhouse I use top-quality local Pennsylvania trout. This dish is not only low in calories but is very colorful, with its golden trout, orange carrot, light green and yellow squash, and the dark green spinach. Accompany this entrée with a plain salad, or a lowfat side dish such as wild rice or quinoa pilaf, and you have a perfect nutritional match.

VINAIGRETTE

$^1/_2$ cup freshly squeezed orange juice or frozen orange juice concentrate

$^1/_4$ cup white wine vinegar

2 teaspoons minced shallots

$^1/_2$ cup olive oil

TROUT

2 teaspoons olive oil

4 skinless fresh trout, heads removed (about 6 ounces each), cut into 2 fillets each

Freshly cracked black pepper

PARISIAN VEGETABLES

$^1/_2$ carrot

$^1/_2$ zucchini

$^1/_2$ yellow squash

1 ounce fresh spinach (about $^3/_4$ cup, firmly packed)

2 tablespoons julienned fresh basil, for garnish

To prepare the vinaigrette, place the orange juice, vinegar, and shallots in a blender and purée until smooth. Gradually add the olive oil in a steady stream, blending until emulsified. Set aside.

To prepare the trout, heat 1 teaspoon of the olive oil in a sauté pan. Season the trout with the black pepper. Cooking 2 of the fillets at a time in the hot pan, sauté over medium-high heat for 3 to 4 minutes on each side, until golden brown. Remove from the pan and keep warm. Repeat for the remaining fillets.

To prepare the vegetables, bring a saucepan of water to a boil. Using a Parisian scoop (melon baller), scoop out 12 balls each of the carrot, zucchini, and yellow squash. Blanch the carrots for 3 minutes; blanch the zucchini and yellow squash for $1^1/2$ minutes. Drain, reserving the cooking water, and keep warm.

Bring $^1/2$ cup of the drained cooking water to a boil in a separate pan, add the spinach, and cook for about 1 minute, or until wilted. Strain and mound the spinach at the top and center of each serving plate. Place the trout on the plate, crisscrossing and leaning on the spinach. Ladle 1 tablespoon of the vinaigrette over the trout, and scatter the vegetables around the trout. Garnish with the basil, and serve.

NUTRITIONAL INFORMATION PER SERVING
Total Calories: 308
Total Fat: 14 gm.
Saturated Fat: 2 gm.
Cholesterol: 97 mg.
Sodium: 106 mg.
Fiber Rating: 3 gm.

Lemon Thyme–Marinated Broiled Cod Fillet with Radicchio Salsa and Arugula

SERVES: 4

Cod has a distinctive and delicious rich flavor and a moist, flaky, and clean texture. It is adaptable in the kitchen and can be cooked in all kinds of ways, and is also dried as salt cod, or smoked. The acidic marinade matches the cod well, cutting its richness a little. The peppery arugula and the salsa both have the same effect. I like to use lemon thyme, as it combines robustly aromatic herbal qualities with a delicate lemon flavor that works well with most fish. If unavailable, use regular thyme with a squeeze of lemon.

MARINADE

1 cup olive oil

$^1/_2$ cup red wine vinegar

1 tablespoon minced fresh lemon thyme

1 tablespoon coriander seeds

1 tablespoon chopped garlic

1 tablespoon chopped shallots

4 boneless, skinless cod fillets, about 6 ounces each

RADICCHIO SALSA

$^1/_4$ cup packed julienned radicchio

2 tablespoons peeled, cored, seeded, and diced apple

1 tablespoon seeded and diced green bell pepper

1 teaspoon chopped cilantro

$^1/_4$ cup balsamic vinegar

1 tablespoon honey

$^1/_4$ teaspoon salt

$^1/_4$ cup bread crumbs

ARUGULA

4 ounces arugula (about $2^1/_4$ cups, firmly packed)

Juice of 1 lemon

1 teaspoon olive oil

Combine all the marinade ingredients in a mixing bowl. Add the cod fillets and let marinate for 2 hours.

Preheat the oven to 450°.

Place all the salsa ingredients in a small saucepan. Bring to a boil over high heat and cook for 2 minutes, stirring occasionally. Remove from the heat and let cool.

Lightly brush off the excess marinade and place the cod in an ovenproof baking dish. Bake in the oven for about 5 minutes, until the fillets begin to flake. Set the broiler to high. Sprinkle 1 tablespoon of the bread crumbs on each fillet, transfer to the broiler, and broil for about 2 minutes, until golden brown on one side.

Place the arugula in a mixing bowl and toss thoroughly with the lemon juice and olive oil. Arrange the tossed arugula at the top of each serving plate, and place one cod fillet in the center of each plate so it rests on a little of the arugula. Serve with the radicchio salsa.

NOTE: Don't be afraid to use the amount of olive oil called for in the marinade. You will brush off most of it before cooking, and, at most, only about 1 teaspoon will remain on each fillet (which is the amount reflected in the nutritional information). Although some marinades can be saved and reused, this marinade should be discarded after one use.

NUTRITIONAL INFORMATION PER SERVING

Total Calories: 225

Total Fat: 7 gm.

Saturated Fat: 1 gm.

Cholesterol: 74 mg.

Sodium: 263 mg.

Fiber Rating: 1 gm.

Pan-Seared Rigatoni with Chicken and Swiss Chard

SERVES: 4

Chicken and turkey are among the most common types of leftovers because people tend to roast whole birds that are not necessarily eaten at one sitting. The good news is that pasta is one of the best mediums for leftover poultry. I particularly like the macaroni-like rigatoni pasta because it crisps well— we've done plenty of research in the Rittenhouse kitchen, and we've found that it crisps better than any other pasta. The advantage of a crisp pasta as called for in this recipe is that it contrasts well with the smooth textures of the other ingredients, and especially with the chard. Swiss chard is a late winter, spring, and early summer vegetable, but it says "April" to me. Chard is related to beetroot, and if you can find ruby Swiss chard (also called rhubarb chard), you'll be able to serve a visual, as well as a taste, treat. I grow ruby chard in my garden at home, and it looks beautiful even if you never plan to eat it.

1 pound dried rigatoni

2 teaspoons olive oil

1 pound boneless, skinless chicken breast, cut into strips

1 pound Swiss chard, stemmed

2 tablespoons minced garlic

1 red bell pepper, seeded and julienned

1 teaspoon minced shallots

2 cups Low-Sodium Chicken Stock (page 225)

Salt and freshly cracked black pepper to taste

4 scallions, green portion only, finely sliced

Bring a saucepan of salted water to a boil. Add the rigatoni, return to a boil, and cook for 8 to 12 minutes, until tender. Drain and set aside.

Heat a large nonstick sauté pan coated with nonstick cooking spray and add 1 teaspoon of the olive oil. Add the chicken to the hot pan and sauté over medium-high heat for about 3 minutes, until cooked through and golden brown. Remove the chicken from the pan and set aside.

Wipe the pan clean and heat the remaining 1 teaspoon olive oil. Add the rigatoni to the hot pan and cook over medium-high heat for 2 to 3 minutes, until crisp and lightly browned. Add the cooked chicken, Swiss chard, garlic, bell pepper, shallots, and stock, and cook for 3 minutes. Season with salt and pepper and cook for 2 minutes longer, or until nicely glazed. Add the scallions, toss together, and transfer to serving bowls.

NOTE: For fewer calories, reduce the amount of pasta per serving.

NUTRITIONAL INFORMATION PER SERVING

Total Calories: 648

Total Fat: 14 gm.

Saturated Fat: 3 gm.

Cholesterol: 52 mg.

Sodium: 783 mg.

Fiber Rating: 2 gm.

Chicken and Turkey Sausage Cassoulet with Three-Bean Ragout

SERVES: 4

I love making sausages. Once you get the hang of it, it's easy, and best of all, it's fun. It's certainly a lot less intimidating than most people think, especially if you use plastic wrap, as in this recipe, rather than traditional sausage casings. I get my kids to help with the sausages; they love it, and it makes an interesting alternative to Play-Doh. Not only that, but they get to eat the results, so they're happy. It seems as though it's when baseball season rolls around that sausage season begins, and time to start thinking of cookouts. Nothing goes better with sausages than beans, so pairing them in a cassoulet makes perfect sense. The tradition of cassoulets comes from southern France, where white beans are cooked slowly in a casserole with sausage, pork, duck, or goose, or with a braising meat. Be sure to cook the different types of beans separately, as they have different cooking times. It's important to never bring the beans to a full boil, but just to simmer them until tender. Avoid adding salt to the beans while they are cooking, as this will make them tough and indigestible.

RAGOUT

$^2/_3$ cup dried black beans, rinsed and soaked overnight

$^2/_3$ cup dried kidney beans, rinsed and soaked overnight

$^2/_3$ cup dried white beans, rinsed and soaked overnight

1 teaspoon olive oil

1 tablespoon chopped garlic

$^1/_2$ onion, diced

$^1/_2$ tablespoon chopped shallots

1 cup Low-Sodium Chicken Stock (page 225)

1 large tomato, blanched, peeled, seeded, and diced

1 tablespoon ground cumin

1 teaspoon dried sage

1 tablespoon chopped fresh thyme

1 tablespoon chopped fresh parsley

$^1/_2$ teaspoon salt

SAUSAGE

SERVES: 4

6 ounces ground chicken breast

6 ounces ground turkey breast

1 1/2 tablespoons chopped garlic

1 tablespoon chopped shallots

1/2 teaspoon dried sage

1/2 teaspoon ground cumin

1 tablespoon dried thyme

1 teaspoon dried mustard powder

1/4 teaspoon freshly grated nutmeg

2 tablespoons chopped fresh parsley

2 teaspoons freshly ground black pepper

1 egg white

8 sprigs each of thyme, sage, flat-leaf parsley and chives (or other herbs), for garnish

2 tomatoes, quartered, seeded, pulp removed, and julienned into 24 to 32 strips for garnish (optional)

To prepare the ragout, drain and rinse the beans and put them into separate saucepans. Cover with about 1 inch of fresh water and bring to a boil over high heat. Reduce the heat to a simmer and cook the beans for about 45 minutes, or until tender. Drain and set aside.

Heat the olive oil in a sauté pan. Add the garlic, onion, and shallots, and sauté over medium heat for 2 to 3 minutes. Stir in the cooked beans and remaining ragout ingredients over medium-high heat; reduce by half. Remove from the heat and keep warm.

Thoroughly combine all the sausage ingredients in a mixing bowl. Place 4 sheets of plastic wrap each measuring 12 inches square separately on a flat surface. Divide the sausage mixture into 4 equal portions and place a portion in the center of each plastic sheet. Using your hands, form the sausage into an oblong shape, about 6 inches long and 3/4 to 1 inch wide. Fold the bottom of each piece of plastic wrap over the sausage to cover. Lightly press the sausage into a cylinder shape and continue to roll up all of the plastic. Twist the ends of the plastic wrap so they form tight rolls. Set aside.

Bring at least 2 quarts of water to a boil in a large saucepan. Place the sausages in the boiling water and poach over medium heat for about 5 minutes, or until they harden, set, and are firm to the touch. Remove the sausages from the water and let cool. When cool, remove the plastic wrap and discard.

Coat a nonstick sauté pan with nonstick cooking spray and place over medium-high heat. Add the poached sausages and sauté for 2 to 3 minutes, constantly shaking the pan to brown on all sides.

Spoon the bean ragout onto serving plates. Slice each sausage into 3 sections, placing them upright at the top of each plate (in the 12 o'clock position). Using 2 sprigs of each herb garnish per serving, gather into a bunch and place upright on top of the sausage. Spoon the ragout at the foot of the sausage and across the plate. Garnish the top of the ragout with the tomato strips. Serve immediately.

NOTE: You can use either chicken or turkey, rather than both, if you prefer. Ground chicken is more easily available and has a smoother texture, while ground turkey is coarser, which I prefer for sausage making. Be sure to buy ground turkey breast, because packets labeled "ground turkey" are likely to include the fattier dark meat and skin.

NUTRITIONAL INFORMATION PER SERVING

Total Calories: 329

Total Fat: 5 gm.

Saturated Fat: 1 gm.

Cholesterol: 71 mg.

Sodium: 114 mg.

Fiber Rating: 25 gm.

Sautéed Lamb Scaloppine with Green Peppercorn Minted Jus

SERVES: 4

Lamb is probably the quintessential spring meat, and lamb and mint are classic partners. Yes, spring is in the air with this recipe! Some people think of lamb as a little gamey and strong tasting, but a lot of that flavor is in the fat. Here, we carefully trim the fat from the lamb, so all you'll get is the succulent flavor of the tender lamb meat. Many lamb dishes, such as scaloppine and piccata, are interchangeable with veal, and vice versa.

LAMB

4 lamb scaloppines (taken from the leg or loin), trimmed of all fat and pounded, about 5 ounces each

Flour for dredging

Freshly ground black pepper to taste

1 tablespoon olive oil

GREEN PEPPERCORN MINTED JUS

1 tablespoon brandy

1 tablespoon chopped shallots

1 tomato, blanched, peeled, seeded, and diced

1 cup Lamb Stock (page 228)

1 tablespoon chopped fresh mint

1 tablespoon green peppercorns

1 tablespoon freshly squeezed lemon juice

$1/2$ teaspoon salt

4 mint sprigs for garnish

Dredge the lamb scaloppines in the flour to lightly coat; shake off the excess flour. Season with the black pepper. Heat the olive oil in a nonstick sauté pan. Add the scaloppines to the hot pan and sauté over medium-high heat for about 1 minute on each side, until browned. Remove the lamb from the pan and keep warm.

To prepare the jus, deglaze the pan with the brandy. Add the shallots, tomato, lamb stock, mint, green peppercorns, lemon juice, and salt; reduce by half.

Spoon the jus onto the plate in a crescent shape, following the rim of the plate. Place the lamb scaloppines so they overlap half of the jus, tracing the inside contour of the crescent. Garnish the center of each plate with a mint sprig, and serve. Serve with couscous or oven-roasted potatoes, if desired.

NOTE: Don't hesitate to ask your butcher for the leanest lamb scaloppines available. The leanest cuts of lamb are leg, shoulder, and loin, but even so, it is important to trim away all visible fat from the meat. Lean lamb is a little lower in cholesterol than beef, pork, or veal, but it is moderately high in fat compared to chicken, so eat it only occasionally and in small amounts.

NUTRITIONAL INFORMATION PER SERVING:
Total Calories: 319
Total Fat: 14 gm.
Saturated Fat: 4 gm.
Cholesterol: 126 mg.
Sodium: 345 mg.
Fiber Rating: 0.4 gm.

Stir-Fried Pork Loin with Crispy Vegetable Lo Mein

This light, refreshing style of meal is perfect for spring. When the farm stands start opening up for business in May, when farmers' markets start up again, or when stores start selling fresh seasonal spring produce again, think of making this dish. lo mein are dark brown, wheat noodles that resemble spaghetti (which you can substitute for lo mein if necessary). When I was growing up, this is the kind of Chinese-meets-American meal my mother would make. Among the features she undoubtedly enjoyed in this recipe was that it was simple and could be cooked in a single pan. This version is almost a Southern version of Chinese lo mein, but whatever the culinary style, stir-frying fresh vegetables to cook them crisply is a very healthy technique.

SERVES: 4

20 ounces boneless, skinless pork loin, trimmed of all fat, cut into 2-inch-thick slices

Arrowroot or cornstarch for dredging

1 tablespoon canola oil

1/2 onion, sliced

2 tablespoons chopped garlic

8 large domestic or shiitake mushrooms, sliced

1 carrot, julienned

1 zucchini, julienned

1 yellow squash, julienned

5 or 6 scallions, white and green portions, chopped

12 snow peas

1 cup Low-Sodium Chicken Stock (page 225)

2 tablespoons low-sodium soy sauce

8 ounces lomein noodles, cooked, drained, and cooled

2 tablespoons freshly squeezed lemon juice

2 teaspoons crushed red pepper flakes

2 tablespoons chopped fresh cilantro

4 large cilantro sprigs, for garnish

NUTRITIONAL
INFORMATION PER
SERVING

Total Calories: 309

Total Fat: 9 gm.

Saturated Fat: 2 gm.

Cholesterol: 101 mg.

Sodium: 417 mg.

Fiber Rating: 3 gm

Dredge the pork strips in the arrowroot or cornstarch to lightly coat; shake off any excess. Heat the canola oil in a sauté pan. Add the pork to the hot pan and stir-fry over medium-high heat for about 2 minutes. Immediately add the onion and garlic, and stir-fry for about 2 minutes, until the pork and onion are brown.

Add the mushrooms, carrots, zucchini, yellow squash, scallions, snow peas, chicken stock, and soy sauce, and toss together. Stir-fry for 2 to 3 minutes, then add the noodles, toss again, and stir-fry for 1 minute more. Add the lemon juice, crushed red pepper flakes, cilantro, and toss to combine. Heat thoroughly for 1 or 2 minutes, until the liquid thickens.

Divide the stir-fry ingredients between serving bowls, garnish with the cilantro sprigs, and serve immediately.

NOTE: Most of the sodium comes from the soy sauce. If you are concerned with sodium levels, omit the soy sauce. Pork tenderloin compares well to chicken in terms of fat. A 3-ounce portion of trimmed, roasted pork tenderloin contains only 4.1 grams of total fat and 1.4 grams of saturated fat, compared to 3 ounces of chicken breast, which has 3.0 grams of total fat and 0.9 grams of saturated fat.

Thyme and Yogurt Crème Brûlée with Spicy Caramelized Oranges

This dessert is the lowfat equivalent of a traditional brûlée, and it is supremely smooth and delicious. It simulates the feel of a rich egg custard by using yogurt cheese, a nonfat yogurt that does not have gelatin added to it. By draining nonfat yogurt in a cheesecloth-lined colander overnight, the excess liquid is removed and a "cheese" is formed (you can also use a coffee filter). You will lose about 25 percent of the volume after the draining process, so 2 pints of yogurt is necessary to yield $1^1/2$ pounds of yogurt cheese. In this recipe, the oranges act as a refreshing foil for the richness of the custard. Herbs are rarely used in desserts (this may be changing—you can buy basil chocolate now), but they can highlight and complement sweet flavors.

SERVES: 6

BRÛLÉE

$1^1/2$ pounds yogurt cheese

3 tablespoons nonfat cream cheese

$^3/4$ cup sugar

$^1/2$ teaspoon minced fresh thyme or dill

Minced zest of $^1/2$ orange

$^1/2$ teaspoon pure vanilla extract

$^2/3$ cup egg substitute (such as Eggbeaters)

6 thyme sprigs, for garnish

SPICY CARAMELIZED ORANGES

3 large oranges, peeled and sectioned

$^1/4$ teaspoon ground cardamom

$^1/8$ teaspoon ground mace

3 tablespoons sugar

Preheat the oven to 325°.

To prepare the brûlées, cream together the yogurt cheese and cream cheese in a mixing bowl with a rubber spatula until smooth. Blend in the sugar, thyme, orange zest, and vanilla until smooth. Stir in the egg substitute, a little at a time, until fully incorporated. Divide the mixture between 6 four-ounce ramekins, and place in a water bath (bain marie).

Bake in the oven for 20 minutes, or until firm to the touch. Remove from the oven and let cool. Refrigerate for about 1 hour, until completely chilled.

To prepare the caramelized oranges, combine the orange sections, cardamom, mace, and sugar in a mixing bowl. Cover and let marinate for at least 10 minutes.

When you are ready to serve, drain the oranges and arrange 5 sections on top of each brûlée. Sprinkle $1/2$ tablespoon of the sugar over each brûlée and place under a hot broiler to caramelize; be careful not to burn the top. Garnish with the thyme sprigs.

NOTE: Yogurt is a wonderfully versatile food. It can be used as a snack or recipe ingredient. It stands on its own in terms of flavor, and it readily combines with savory or sweet flavors. Eating one cup of nonfat yogurt every day helps meet the daily nutritional requirements for vitamins B_{12} and D.

NUTRITIONAL INFORMATION PER SERVING

Total Calories: 259

Total Fat: 1 gm.

Saturated Fat: 0.4 gm.

Cholesterol: 4 mg.

Sodium: 215 mg.

Fiber Rating: 1 gm.

Three-Melon Dessert Soup with Candied Ginger Sherbet

SERVES: 4

*M*ark Twain wrote that watermelons are one of the world's great luxuries, and that tasting watermelon gives us an idea of what angels eat! This is a very refreshing dessert that is particularly welcome after a filling meal, or one that features heavier flavors, such as red meat. Melons were always a big treat when I was growing up, but because they took up too much room in the refrigerator, my parents rarely bought them. One of the many good things about melons is that their quality is usually consistent, even in spring when produce markets work a balancing act between California, Florida, and foreign produce, resulting in a mixed bag when it comes to quality. This makes melons a reliable, "quick fix" dessert that both satisfies the sweet tooth and refreshes the palate. Most dessert soup recipes call for a cooked sugar-syrup base which is then flavored. You must take special precaution when using this method for fruits with a high water content, as the hot liquid tends to destroy the subtle flavors of this type of produce. Instead, cool or refrigerate the simple syrup before adding any purée.

SOUP

1 small honeydew melon

1 large cantaloupe melon

1 cup seedless watermelon (scooped from 1 small wedge)

$^{1}/_{3}$ cup white wine

$^{1}/_{4}$ cup sugar

$^{1}/_{2}$ vanilla bean, split in half lengthwise and seeds scraped

Minced zest of $^{1}/_{2}$ lemon

$^{1}/_{4}$ teaspoon freshly grated nutmeg

SOUR CREAM SAUCE

$^{1}/_{4}$ cup nonfat sour cream

$1^{1}/_{2}$ tablespoons sugar

Juice of 1 lime

CANDIED GINGER SHERBET

2 cups water

2 tablespoons minced candied ginger

$^{1}/_{2}$ cup lowfat (1%) milk

$^{1}/_{2}$ cup sugar

$^{1}/_{2}$ vanilla bean, split in half lengthwise and seeds scraped

To prepare the soup, scoop eighteen balls out of the flesh of the honey-dew and cantaloupe melons with a melon baller or scoop. Place the melon balls and watermelon in a food processor or blender and purée until smooth. Add the white wine, sugar, vanilla seeds and bean, lemon zest, and nutmeg, and purée until thoroughly incorporated. Set aside.

To prepare the sauce, mix together the sour cream, sugar, and lime juice in a mixing bowl. Set aside.

To prepare the sherbet, place the water and candied ginger in a saucepan. Bring to a boil over high heat, and reduce by half. Stir in the milk, sugar, and vanilla seeds and bean; remove from the heat and let cool. Pour the mixture into an ice-cream maker and freeze according to the manufacturer's directions.

To serve, spoon the soup into serving bowls and top with a couple of scoops of the sherbet. Garnish by drizzling the sauce around the sherbet.

NOTE: Melons are mainly composed of water (watermelon is 92 percent water). There are only 60 calories in $1^{1}/_{4}$ cups of watermelon, about the same number as in half of a 5-inch honeydew melon (about 1 cup). Cantaloupe is an excellent source of vitamins A and C and the antioxidant beta-carotene.

NUTRITIONAL
INFORMATION PER
SERVING

Total Calories: 358

Total Fat: 1 gm.

Saturated Fat: 0.2 gm.

Cholesterol: 1 mg.

Sodium: 78 mg.

Fiber Rating: 4 gm.

Pineapple and Sage Macaroon Tart with Honey-Vinegar Syrup and Frozen Nutmeg Yogurt

SERVES: 8
(ONE 8-INCH
TART)

This is a firm favorite at the Rittenhouse. The tartness of the pineapple is balanced by the sweetness of the macaroons—a classic combination of sweet and sour—and the frozen yogurt caps it all off perfectly. The frozen yogurt will go with almost anything, and best of all, it's fat-free. The day before preparing the tart, cut the leaves off the pineapple and invert it on the counter overnight. This will allow the juice to repermeate the entire fruit instead of just collecting in the bottom half.

MACAROON BASE

6 ounces (³/₄ cup) almond paste

2 egg whites

PINEAPPLE

1 pineapple, peeled, cored, and sliced into ¹/₂-inch-thick rings (about 8 to 12 rings)

SYRUP

1 cup sugar

¹/₂ cup water

2 tablespoons honey

¹/₄ cup unseasoned rice wine vinegar

FROZEN NUTMEG YOGURT

2 cups nonfat yogurt

¹/₃ cup all-fruit peach preserves

¹/₂ tablespoon freshly grated nutmeg

1 tablespoon minced fresh sage

Preheat the oven to 325°.

To prepare the macaroon base, place the almond paste and 1 of the egg whites in the bowl of a heavy-duty electric mixer and cream together with a wooden spoon until smooth. With the mixer on medium speed, beat in the remaining egg white until soft and smooth.

Pour the batter on a nonstick baking sheet and spread out with a spatula to form an 8-inch circle. Par-bake in the oven for about 8 minutes, or until it begins to brown. Remove from the oven and let cool.

Place the pineapple rings in a large mixing bowl and set aside.

To prepare the syrup, place the sugar, water, honey, and vinegar in a small saucepan. Bring to a boil, stirring constantly, until the sugar has dissolved. Remove from the heat and pour over the pineapple rings. Let marinate for 15 minutes, until cooled.

Remove the pineapple rings from the syrup and reserve 2 of the rings for the frozen yogurt. Reserve the syrup. Arrange the remaining rings on the almond crust, covering it in a single layer. Bake them in the oven for another 20 minutes, until the crust is golden brown.

To prepare the frozen yogurt, place the 2 reserved pineapple rings in a food processor or blender and purée until smooth. Transfer to a mixing bowl and add the yogurt, peach preserves, and nutmeg, and mix together thoroughly. Pour the mixture into an ice-cream maker and freeze according to the manufacturer's directions.

Place the reserved syrup in a saucepan and bring to a boil. Reduce the heat and simmer for 3 minutes. Stir in the sage. Remove from the heat, and keep warm.

To serve, cut the tart into 8 pieces. Place 1 piece on each plate and cover with the warm syrup. Top with a scoop of the frozen yogurt, and serve.

NUTRITIONAL
INFORMATION PER
SERVING

Total Calories: 326

Total Fat: 6.6 gm.

Saturated Fat: 0.8 gm.

Cholesterol: 1.0 gm.

Sodium: 61 mg.

Fiber Rating: 1.4 gm.

Tarragon Chilean Cherry Clafouti with Burnt Sugar Parfait and Cabernet Glaze

SERVES: 8

Chilean fruit, such as citrus, berries, stone fruit, and apples, continues to improve in quality annually. The arrival of this bounty usually gives us the first signs that our own spring produce is on its way. Because Chile is in the Southern Hemisphere and their seasons are the opposite of ours, the fruits we get from Chile in the spring are usually those we associate with fall. There is no better way to show off the exceptional Chilean cherry harvest than in the classic French pastry clafouti, which originates from the Limousin region. Clafouti is basically a custard tart with an unusual firmness because of the added flour.

CLAFOUTI

1 cup sugar

3/4 cup egg substitute (such as Eggbeaters)

Juice and minced zest of 2 oranges

1/2 cup all-purpose flour

2/3 cup fat-free margarine

1 1/2 tablespoons minced fresh tarragon

1 1/2 cups fresh pitted cherries (about 35 to 40)

PARFAIT

1/3 cup sugar

1 tablespoon hot water

4 ounces (about 1/2 cup) nonfat cream cheese

3 egg whites

1 tablespoon pure vanilla extract

CABERNET GLAZE

1/2 tablespoon cornstarch

1 1/4 cups Cabernet Sauvignon

1 1/2 tablespoons sugar

1/4 cup chopped and pitted fresh cherries (about 6)

Preheat the oven to 350°.

To prepare the clafouti, mix together the sugar, egg substitute, orange juice, and zest in a mixing bowl. Set aside. Melt the margarine in a saucepan, stir in the tarragon, and cook over medium heat for about 1 minute. Remove from the heat. Gradually stir in a little of the flour and then a little of the margarine mixture into the sugar-egg mixture, alternating each, and mix until smooth. Spray an 8-inch pound cake pan with nonstick cooking spray and pour the batter into it. Add the cherries, and bake in the oven for about 1 hour, or until firm to the touch. Remove from the oven and turn out onto a rack to cool.

To prepare the parfait, place the sugar in a sauté pan and caramelize over medium-high heat, until dark amber in color. Stir in the hot water until incorporated, and then remove the pan from the heat. Stir in the cream cheese until the mixture is smooth, and set aside to cool.

In a mixing bowl, beat the egg whites to soft peaks. Fold the cooled sugar mixture into the egg whites and stir in the vanilla. Spoon the mixture into muffin pans lined with paper muffin cups and freeze for about 2 hours, until solid.

To prepare the glaze, mix together the cornstarch and $1/4$ cup of the wine in a mixing bowl, until dissolved. Place the remaining wine in a saucepan and bring to a boil. Stir in the cornstarch mixture and cook for about 2 minutes, until the mixture turns clear. Stir in the sugar and the $1/4$ cup cherries, and cook for 1 to 2 minutes, until the sugar dissolves and the cherries are heated through. Keep warm.

Cut the clafouti into 8 pieces, and slice each piece in half again. Remove the parfait from the freezer and peel off the paper liners. Stack 2 slices of the clafouti on top of each parfait, and pour the warm Cabernet Glaze over the tart. The texture of the clafouti will be very firm when cooled to room temperature, but it will become undesirably hard if refrigerated. Store covered at room temperature until ready to eat, or serve immediately.

NUTRITIONAL INFORMATION PER SERVING:

Total Calories: 351

Total Fat: 1 gm.

Saturated Fat: 0.3 gm.

Cholesterol: 4 mg.

Sodium: 450 mg.

Fiber Rating: 1 gm.

Summer

APPETIZERS

Marinated Vegetable Roulade with Spicy Dipping Sauce / 58
Alaskan Salmon and Spinach Lasagna / 61
Tomato and Cucumber Gazpacho with Lime Yogurt / 63
Crab and Roasted Pepper Quesadillas with Pico de Gallo Salsa / 64

SALADS

Ruby Grapefruit and Black Bean Salad / 66
Scallop Ceviche and Avocado Salad / 69
Smoked Trout, Cucumber, and Mâche Salad with Mustard Seed Vinaigrette / 70
Charred Asparagus Salad with Tomato and Mixed Greens / 72

ENTRÉES

*Oven-Roasted Beefsteak Tomato, Spinach, and Zucchini Napoleon
with Roasted Red Pepper Coulis / 75*
Poached Halibut and Lemon Couscous with Citrus Vinaigrette / 77
Pan-Seared Scallops with Tomato Fettucine, Snow Peas, and Water Chestnuts / 79
Gulf Shrimp Stir-Fry with Bok Choy, Mushrooms, and a Trio of Peppers / 81
Grilled Chicken Breast with Melon Salsa and Tortilla and Arugula Salad / 83
Turkey Fajitas with Peppers and Onions and Summer Vegetable Escabeche / 86
Caraway-Crusted Pork Medallions with Vine-Ripened Tomatoes and Red Onions / 88
Lemongrass-Marinated Filet Mignon with Oven-Baked Chile Potato Chips / 90

DESSERTS

Stir-Fried Tropical Fruit Napoleon with Sesame Seed Meringues / 92
Black Plum and Sour Cream Tart with Oatmeal Streusel / 95
Phyllo Basket with Lemongrass Sherbet and Raspberry-Peach Compote / 97
Blueberry and Port Cobbler with Sweet Potato Dumpling Crust / 99

Opposite: Caraway-Crusted Pork Medallions with Vine-Ripened Tomatoes and Red Onions, page 88.

Marinated Vegetable Roulade with Spicy Dipping Sauce

SERVES: 4

his low-calorie starter has been a popular summertime item at the Rittenhouse. It's light, refreshing, and won't fill you up, but it's full of flavor—the perfect appetizer. "Roulade" is the culinary term for a rolled ingredient (usually meat) that holds a filling (usually vegetables), but in this case, the entire dish is vegetarian. The selection of ingredients for the filling echoes the ingredients of Asian spring rolls, and you can switch them around to suit your taste or the availability of produce. For example, you can use daikon, radish, or jicama, green or yellow zucchini, asparagus, or mushrooms; the only limit is your own creativity!

MARINADE AND DIPPING SAUCE

$1/4$ cup unseasoned rice wine vinegar

$1^1/2$ tablespoons sugar

$1/4$ teaspoon red pepper flakes, or more to taste

2 cloves garlic, minced

FILLING

1 cup bean sprouts

1 cup shredded Chinese cabbage

$1/2$ cup julienned carrots

$1/4$ cup thinly sliced canned water chestnuts

WRAPPING

4 large Chinese cabbage leaves

Combine the marinade ingredients in a mixing bowl. Add the filling ingredients and marinate for at least 1 hour.

Meanwhile, bring a saucepan of water to a boil and blanch the cabbage leaves for about 1 minute, until wilted. Remove from the pan and immediately place in an ice water bath to cool. Drain, and place on paper towels to dry.

Remove the filling ingredients from the marinade, drain well, and reserve the marinade. Lay the blanched cabbage leaves out on a work surface with the stem end facing away from you and the leafy green part toward you. Spoon the filling onto the leafy end of the cabbage leaves and roll the cabbage leaves up towards the stem end, until the mixture is enclosed. Fold the sides of the leaves in and continue rolling up, until completely wrapped.

Place a roulade on each serving plate and serve the marinade as a dipping sauce on the side in small cups or ramekins.

NOTE: Vinegar is a wonderful ingredient. It is low in calories, sodium, sugar, and fat, and it is high in flavor. Rice wine vinegar has a sharp but fresh, uncomplicated flavor that is not as acidic as regular distilled vinegar. All types of vinegar make a healthful seasoning substitute for salt.

NUTRITIONAL INFORMATION PER SERVING

Total Calories: 52

Total Fat: 0 gm.

Saturated Fat: 0 gm.

Cholesterol: 0 mg.

Sodium: 19 mg.

Fiber Rating: 2 gm.

Alaskan Salmon and Spinach Lasagna

*M*y very first cooking job was at an Italian restaurant in Dallas, where we served prodigious amounts of lasagna. At the end of the evening I'd be covered in tomato sauce, but I became a lasagna maven. Since then, I have learned to look for excuses to create all kinds of different lasagnas, and this is one of my favorites. It's a great way to use up leftover salmon—even smoked salmon—or less expensive salmon end cuts. The flavor of the fish is strong enough that it won't get lost among the other ingredients. You can easily double this recipe and serve it as an entrée.

SERVES: 4

POACHING BROTH

$^1/_2$ cup white wine

$^1/_2$ cup clam juice

1 teaspoon minced shallots

1 teaspoon minced garlic

5 black peppercorns

1 clove

14 ounces salmon

5 sheets dried lasagna pasta

TOMATO SAUCE

2 cups chopped canned plum
  tomatoes, liquid reserved

$1^1/_2$ tablespoons minced garlic

$1^1/_2$ tablespoons chopped shallots

3 tablespoons minced fresh basil

2 tablespoons minced fresh oregano

$^1/_2$ tablespoon minced fresh parsley

FILLING

$1^1/_2$ cups nonfat ricotta cheese

2 cups fresh spinach leaves

Freshly cracked black pepper to taste

8 plum tomatoes or 2 large tomatoes,
  seeded and finely diced, for garnish
  (optional)

4 sprigs dill, for garnish

Combine all the broth ingredients in a saucepan and bring to a boil. Reduce the heat to a light simmer, add the salmon, and poach for 5 to 8 minutes, depending on the thickness of the fish. Remove the salmon from the broth and transfer on a plate to the refrigerator. When cold, flake the salmon into large pieces with a fork and set aside.

Bring a large saucepan of water to a boil. Add the lasagna sheets and cook for 2 to 3 minutes, until al dente. Drain and place in a cold water bath to cool.

Preheat the oven to 350°.

Combine all the ingredients for the tomato sauce in a mixing bowl. Spread a thin layer of the tomato sauce in the bottom of a 9 x 6-inch lasagna pan or baking pan. Follow, in order, with layers of the pasta, ricotta cheese, spinach, and the salmon. Repeat these layers four times, beginning with the tomato sauce; reserve about one-third of the tomato sauce for the top.

Cover the top of the pan tightly with plastic wrap, then cover the plastic wrap with aluminum foil. (The lasagna is covered with both plastic wrap and aluminum foil for cooking because foil should never be placed directly over food containing acid, as it is reactive. Since the plastic wrap is covered by the foil, it will not melt.) Bake in the oven for 30 minutes. Remove from the oven and cut into slices. Alternatively, using a round cutter, cut the lasagna into circles. Place a piece in the center of each plate.

Cut off the tops and bottoms off the plum tomatoes and stand the remainder on a work surface. Cut four thin strips off the outer flesh and skin each tomato, cutting downwards. Cut a diamond shape from each strip and place 8 tomato diamonds around the lasagna on each plate. Alternatively, sprinkle the diced tomato around the lasagna. Garnish each serving of lasagna with a dill sprig and serve immediately.

NUTRITIONAL
INFORMATION PER
SERVING

Total Calories: 367

Total Fat: 7 gm.

Saturated Fat: 1 gm.

Cholesterol: 55 mg.

Sodium: 429 mg.

Fiber Rating: 2 gm.

Tomato and Cucumber Gazpacho with Lime Yogurt

Gazpacho is the traditional Spanish cold soup. Before the discovery of the New World, the soup was made with almonds introduced to Spain by the Moors. With jalapeños and Tabasco, this recipe has a pleasant zip to it.

SERVES: 4

GAZPACHO

3 cucumbers, peeled, seeded, and coarsely chopped

5 ripe tomatoes, cored and cut in quarters

2 cups V-8 juice

2 tablespoons chopped garlic

1 tablespoon Tabasco

1 large fresh jalapeño chile, seeded and chopped

1 red bell pepper, seeded and chopped

1 green bell pepper, seeded and chopped

¼ cup coarsely chopped fresh cilantro

½ onion, chopped

2 tablespoons freshly squeezed lemon juice

1 tablespoon freshly squeezed lime juice

Freshly ground black pepper to taste

LIME YOGURT

¼ cup nonfat plain yogurt

Juice of 4 freshly squeezed limes

4 sprigs cilantro, for garnish

½ teaspoon minced lime zest, for garnish

NUTRITIONAL INFORMATION PER SERVING

Total Calories: 115

Total Fat: 1 gm.

Saturated Fat: 0.2 mg.

Cholesterol: 0.3 mg.

Sodium: 489 mg.

Fiber Rating: 7 gm.

Place all the gazpacho ingredients in a blender or food processor and purée until smooth but still a little chunky. Refrigerate for 2 hours before serving.

To prepare the lime yogurt, thoroughly mix the yogurt and lime juice together in a mixing bowl. Refrigerate for at least 15 minutes before serving.

To serve, ladle the soup into serving bowls and top each with 1 tablespoon of the lime yogurt. Garnish each serving with a cilantro sprig and a sprinkling of the lime zest.

Crab and Roasted Pepper Quesadillas with Pico de Gallo Salsa

SERVES: 4

I grew up in Dallas, so I was practically weaned on Tex-Mex food. My family would often eat at El Fenix, a huge Tex-Mex restaurant that served plain cheese quesadillas; it was only some time later that I learned that you could make quesadillas with all kinds of interesting filling ingredients, and I've since made up for lost time! In Philadelphia, we are fortunate to be close to the Chesapeake Bay, one of the prime sources of crab—especially blue crab—in the world. Our guests at the Rittenhouse won't hear of substituting the local product with Dungeness crab, for example, at least not during the summer season. Quesadillas are a very adaptable food. Try using shrimp or chicken instead of the crab, or make it vegetarian.

SALSA

2 tomatoes, blanched, peeled, seeded, and chopped

1 teaspoon chopped fresh cilantro

1 1/2 teaspoons minced garlic

3 tablespoons finely diced onion

1/2 fresh jalapeño chile, seeded and minced

1/2 teaspoon freshly squeezed lime juice, or more to taste

Freshly ground black pepper to taste

QUESADILLAS

4 ounces crabmeat, cleaned

1 large red bell pepper, roasted, peeled, seeded, and julienned (page 231)

1 tablespoon chopped fresh cilantro

1 tablespoon sliced scallions

4 medium flour tortillas

4 ounces lowfat Cheddar or Monterey Jack cheese, grated (about 3/4 cup)

2 fresh jalapeño chiles, seeded and cut into 8 slices each

4 sprigs cilantro, for garnish

Thoroughly combine all the salsa ingredients in a mixing bowl. Set aside or refrigerate for 15 to 30 minutes for the flavors to marry (the salsa will keep in the refrigerator for up to 2 days).

To prepare the quesadillas, combine the crabmeat, bell pepper, cilantro, and scallions in a mixing bowl. Set aside. Lay the tortillas out on a work surface and place 3 tablespoons of the grated cheese on half of each tortilla. Place 2 tablespoons of the crabmeat mixture on top of the cheese, and top with 4 jalapeño slices. Fold the tortillas in half to form a half-moon shape.

Preheat the oven to 200°.

Coat a sauté pan with nonstick cooking spray and place over medium-high heat. Place 1 folded tortilla in the hot pan cheese side down and cook for $1^{1}/_{2}$ to $2^{1}/_{2}$ minutes, until golden brown. Turn the tortilla over and continue cooking for $1^{1}/_{2}$ to 2 minutes. Place the quesadilla on a baking sheet or platter in the oven to keep warm, and prepare the remaining tortillas.

Cut each quesadilla into quarters to form triangles. Arrange the quesadilla triangles around a mound of salsa on each serving plate and garnish with the cilantro sprigs.

NUTRITIONAL INFORMATION PER SERVING

Total Calories: 247

Total Fat: 8 gm.

Saturated Fat: 3 gm.

Cholesterol: 47 mg.

Sodium: 417 mg.

Fiber Rating: 3 gm.

NOTES: This recipe was tested with a lowfat cheese with 70 calories (40 calories from fat) and 3 grams of saturated fat per ounce. Some brands contain only 55 calories or less per ounce. This compares with whole-milk cheeses that have about 100 calories per ounce, with 80 calories or so from fat (half of which is saturated fat). Be aware, however, that some lowfat cheeses have higher levels of sodium than their regular counterparts.

Be sure to use fresh jalapeños rather than the canned or pickled ones, which have higher sodium levels as well as a different flavor.

Ruby Grapefruit and Black Bean Salad

SERVES: 4

It seems strange to think that the grapefruit is an accidental hybrid of the pummelo and orange (or a mutation of the pummelo), first grown in the West Indies less than 200 years ago. Ruby grapefruit are a specialty of the Harlingen Valley of southern Texas, and the particular variety grown there is called Texas Ruby Red. I am not alone in considering them the finest grapefruit grown in the United States, and probably, the world. You can use regular white grapefruit instead and the salad will taste just fine (although you may need to add a little more sugar because the Rubies are so sweet), but it will lose some of its striking appearance. The shiny black beans, the vibrant green of the cilantro and jalapeño, and the red of the onion, tomatoes, and grapefruit make this one of the more colorful salads you'll eat. This salad is typical of south Texas, where pairing fruit with beans is popular.

2 cups dried black beans, rinsed and soaked overnight

4 Ruby Red grapefruit, peeled and sectioned

2 tablespoons freshly squeezed lemon juice

3 tablespoons freshly squeezed lime juice

4 tablespoons chopped fresh cilantro

2 large tomatoes, diced

1 red onion, finely diced

$^{1}/_{4}$ teaspoon salt

1 tablespoon olive oil

1 fresh jalapeño chile, seeded and minced

$^{1}/_{2}$ teaspoon sugar

12 sprigs cilantro, for garnish

Drain and rinse the beans and place in a large saucepan. Add enough cold water to cover the beans by about 1 inch. Bring the beans to a boil over high heat. Reduce the heat to a simmer and cook for 30 to 45 minutes, until tender. Add more water if necessary to keep the beans covered. Drain the beans and let cool.

NUTRITIONAL
INFORMATION PER
SERVING

Total Calories: 341

Total Fat: 5 gm.

Saturated Fat: 1 gm.

Cholesterol: 0 mg.

Sodium: 141 mg.

Fiber Rating: 11 gm.

Coarsely chop 1 of the grapefruit sections and place in a large mixing bowl. Add the cooked beans and all of the remaining ingredients except the remaining grapefruit sections and cilantro sprigs. Toss together gently and thoroughly. Refrigerate for 2 hours.

To serve, place 1 cup of the bean salad in the center of each serving plate. Fan out 9 grapefruit segments around the salad on each plate, positioned at 12 o'clock, 4 o'clock, and 8 o'clock. Garnish each plate with 3 cilantro sprigs, placed between the groups of grapefruit segments.

NOTE: This recipe is a great source of cholesterol-lowering soluble fiber. It also provides a good amount of natural antioxidants found in tomatoes and fruit. Antioxidants negate the oxidizing effects of free radicals, which are unstable molecules that damage healthy cells by combining with them and oxidizing them. Some of the damage caused by these free radicals is believed to be a factor in the development of heart disease. Our bodies produce antioxidants that combine with the free radicals to prevent cell damage. Researchers believe that antioxidants such as vitamins C, E, and beta-carotene that we get from dietary sources may act in the same way.

Scallop Ceviche and Avocado Salad

Ceviches are the Latin American appetizers that contain fresh raw fish or shellfish "cooked" in some type of citric acid-based marinade (the acid works to denature the protein content of the meat). It is imperative that you use only the freshest seafood for ceviches, so only buy scallops from a reliable source (don't even try making ceviches with frozen scallops).

SERVES: 4

MARINADE

Juice of 5 freshly squeezed lemons

Juice of 5 freshly squeezed limes

$1/4$ cup olive oil

2 tablespoons tequila

1 tablespoon sugar

1 teaspoon salt

1 teaspoon freshly ground black pepper

2 tablespoons minced garlic

$1/2$ red onion, minced

4 tablespoons chopped cilantro

SCALLOPS

1 pound large sea scallops, cut in half crosswise to form medallions

AVOCADO SALAD

1 ripe avocado, cut into large cubes

$1/4$ red onion, diced

2 tablespoons chopped cilantro

1 tablespoon freshly squeezed lemon juice

1 tablespoon freshly squeezed lime juice

4 lime wedges, for garnish

4 sprigs cilantro, for garnish

NUTRITIONAL INFORMATION PER SERVING

Total Calories: 195

Total Fat: 9 gm.

Saturated Fat: 1 gm.

Cholesterol: 38 mg.

Sodium: 233 mg.

Fiber Rating: 2 gm.

Combine all the marinade ingredients in a mixing bowl. Add the scallops and marinate for 6 to 12 hours in the refrigerator.

Just before you are ready to serve, thoroughly combine all the salad ingredients in a mixing bowl. Drain the scallops thoroughly and divide between martini or wine glasses (or small serving plates). Top with the salad and garnish each glass with a cilantro sprig and a lime wedge.

Smoked Trout, Cucumber, and Mâche Salad with Mustard Seed Vinaigrette

SERVES: 4

This is another salad that reminds me of growing up in Texas. Every Sunday, after church, my mother would put out salad ingredients such as trout or bass that my father had caught and smoked, as well as ham, hard-boiled eggs, tomatoes, and salad greens (especially watercress), which we would then mix and match. Mâche is a delicate salad green with downy medium-to-dark-blue-green leaves. It's also known as lamb's lettuce or corn salad, because it often grows wild in fields of corn. It has a pleasantly sweet, nutty flavor, and can be served in combination with other salad greens or on its own, as in this recipe. Like most other greens, mâche is low in calories and sodium and a good source of vitamins A and C. Unfortunately, mâche is highly perishable, so use it as soon as possible after buying it; even better, grow some in your garden or in a windowbox. This salad can easily be doubled to make a filling lunch or dinner salad.

MUSTARD SEED VINAIGRETTE

1 tablespoon olive oil

1 tablespoon balsamic vinegar

2 tablespoons Pommery (whole-grain) mustard

1 teaspoon sugar

1 teaspoon minced garlic

1 tablespoon finely sliced fresh chives

Freshly ground black pepper to taste

SALAD

4 boneless and skinless smoked trout fillets, about 2 ounces each

2 cucumbers, peeled, cut in half lengthwise, seeded, and cut into $1/8$-inch-thick slices

2 ounces (about 2 cups) mâche or watercress

Thoroughly whisk together all the vinaigrette ingredients in a mixing bowl and set aside.

Using a fork, flake the trout into medium-sized pieces and place in a mixing bowl. Add the cucumbers and toss with all but 1 tablespoon of the vinaigrette; coat well and set aside. Place the mâche in a separate mixing bowl and toss with the remaining tablespoon of vinaigrette.

To serve, place a mound of the trout and cucumber mixture in the center of each serving plate, and top with the dressed mâche. Add the ground pepper to taste.

~

NOTE: Make sure the trout is smoked without salt (if it is hot-smoked, it does not need to be cured and is much less likely to be salted; if it is cold-smoked, it is likely to have been brined or cured with salt). The fat in this recipe comes mainly from the unsaturated fat in the trout.

NUTRITIONAL
INFORMATION PER
SERVING

Total Calories: 174

Total Fat: 10 gm.

Saturated Fat: 1 gm.

Cholesterol: 40

Sodium: 134 mg.

Fiber Rating: 2 gm

Charred Asparagus Salad with Tomato and Mixed Greens

SERVES: 4

*T*his recipe is a variation of a popular summer salad we prepare at the Rittenhouse for special events. It's simple but striking in its presentation. You can grill the asparagus, if you prefer, or use haricots verts that have been blanched before they are charred. Asparagus is one of those foods that I have always adored; like shrimp, it seems that once I start eating it, there's never enough! I like the sound of a German restaurant I've heard about that only serves dishes containing asparagus in some form. Among the items on the menu were asparagus soup, steamed asparagus (served as an appetizer with beer), and white asparagus grilled with olive oil and garlic. It makes me wonder what asparagus ice cream would taste like!

VINAIGRETTE

1 tablespoon olive oil

2 tablespoons red wine vinegar

$^1/_4$ cup Low-Sodium Chicken Stock (page 225)

1 teaspoon minced shallots

1 teaspoon sugar

1 tablespoon finely sliced fresh chives

SALAD

20 asparagus spears

4 ounces mixed greens, such as arugula, mâche, frisée, mizuna, radicchio, and romaine

1 tomato, blanched, peeled, seeded, and diced, for garnish

Place all the vinaigrette ingredients in a blender and blend until emulsified. Set aside.

Trim the asparagus by bending the spears until they break in the middle; discard the thick end and trim the break neatly with a knife. Coat a nonstick sauté pan with nonstick cooking spray and place over high heat. Add about 10 of the asparagus spears at a time and sauté for 4 to 5 minutes, until charred on all sides. Repeat for the remaining asparagus. Remove from the heat and set aside.

Place the greens in a mixing bowl and toss with three-quarters of the vinaigrette. Place a small mound of the dressed greens at the top of each plate. Fan out the asparagus over the bottom portion of the plate, with the ends slightly touching the greens. Sprinkle the remaining vinaigrette over each plate and garnish with the tomatoes.

NUTRITIONAL
INFORMATION PER
SERVING

Total Calories: 89

Total Fat: 4 gm.

Saturated Fat: 1 gm.

Cholesterol: 0 mg.

Sodium: 12 mg.

Fiber Rating: 3 gm.

NOTE: Asparagus is a member of the lily family (like garlic and onions). It was prized by the Greeks and Romans for its medicinal qualities; they believed it would relieve toothaches and repel bees, thus preventing bee stings. It is a good source of vitamins A and C, and it is low in sodium. One pound contains only 66 calories. Arugula is a great source of calcium—1 ounce contains 45 milligrams, and only 7 calories.

Oven-Roasted Beefsteak Tomato, Spinach, and Zucchini Napoleon with Roasted Red Pepper Coulis

*T*his dish makes a substantial vegetarian main course. There's something about the height and substance of napoleons that fascinates me. It's also colorful, a reminder of the vibrance and bounty of summer produce. You can vary the ingredients according to what looks best at the market; for example, you can substitute arugula for the spinach and yellow squash for the zucchini. A great lunch entrée, or you can reduce the portions and serve it as an appetizer.

SERVES: 4

TOMATOES

2 large beefsteak tomatoes, cut in
$^{1}/_{4}$-inch thick slices

RED PEPPER COULIS

2 red bell peppers, roasted, peeled,
seeded, and chopped (page 231)

1 teaspoon chopped garlic

$^{1}/_{4}$ red onion, chopped

$^{1}/_{3}$ cup Low-Sodium Chicken Stock
(page 225)

Freshly ground black pepper to taste

ZUCCHINI

$^{1}/_{2}$ tablespoon minced garlic

1 teaspoon sliced fresh chives

1 teaspoon chiffonade of fresh basil

Pinch of freshly ground black pepper

2 teaspoons olive oil

1 zucchini, cut on the diagonal into
$^{1}/_{8}$-inch-thick slices

SPINACH

$^{1}/_{2}$ teaspoon olive oil

1 tablespoon minced shallots

$^{1}/_{4}$ teaspoon minced garlic

8 ounces fresh spinach, stemmed
($5^{1}/_{2}$ to 6 cups, firmly packed)

4 rosemary sprigs, for garnish

4 spinach leaves, for garnish
(optional)

Preheat the oven to 350°.

To prepare the tomatoes, spray a roasting rack with nonstick cooking spray and place on a baking sheet. Evenly place the sliced tomatoes on the rack and transfer to the oven. Roast for 30 minutes, or until all the moisture has evaporated from the tomato slices and they are slightly firm. Remove from the oven and set aside.

Combine all the coulis ingredients in a food processor and blend until smooth. Transfer to a bowl and set aside.

To prepare the zucchini, combine the garlic, chives, basil, black pepper, and 1 teaspoon of the olive oil in a mixing bowl. Add the zucchini and let marinate for 15 to 30 minutes. Heat the remaining 1 tablespoon of olive oil in a sauté pan. Add the zucchini mixture and sauté over medium heat for 2 to 4 minutes, until golden brown and tender. Set aside.

To prepare the spinach, heat the olive oil in a sauté pan. Add the shallots and garlic and sauté over high heat for about 1 minute, or until the shallots become translucent. Add the spinach and sauté for about 1 minute, tossing frequently, until wilted. Remove from the pan and let cool. Set aside.

To assemble the napoleon, place a mound of the spinach at the top of each plate. Place 2 slices of the zucchini side by side on top of the spinach and top with 2 slices of tomato, also arranged side by side. Repeat this layering process three times. Garnish the top layer with a rosemary sprig. Ladle the coulis at the bottom of the plate and garnish with a spinach leaf if desired. Serve immediately.

❧

NOTE: Fruits and vegetables are a great, tasty way to boost your fiber intake. Spinach is a particularly good source, and it's a versatile ingredient. One cup of raw spinach contains 1.2 grams of dietary fiber, only 12 calories, and, of course, no fat. It's also an excellent source of vitamins A, B, and C.

NUTRITIONAL INFORMATION PER SERVING

Total Calories: 68

Total Fat: 3 gm.

Saturated Fat: 0.5 gm.

Cholesterol: 0 mg.

Sodium: 52 mg.

Fiber Rating: 4 gm.

Poached Halibut and Lemon Couscous with Citrus Vinaigrette

*H*alibut is another favorite fish of mine that is underutilized, which seems a shame as it's highly versatile—it can be grilled, broiled, poached, or sautéed. The wonderful fresh Alaskan halibut that's available in the summer is intensely flavorful and yields almost steak-like meat that makes great fillets. The light, lemon-flavored couscous is the perfect vehicle for balancing the citrusy vinaigrette and the rich halibut. Many people assume that preparing couscous is exotic and difficult, but it's one of the simplest starches to prepare: if you can boil water, you can make couscous!

SERVES: 4

VINAIGRETTE

1¹/₂ tablespoons freshly squeezed lemon juice

1¹/₂ tablespoons freshly squeezed lime juice

1¹/₂ tablespoons freshly squeezed orange juice

¹/₂ tablespoon minced shallots

2 teaspoons finely sliced fresh chives

¹/₂ teaspoon sugar

¹/₂ tablespoon olive oil

LEMON COUSCOUS

1 cup Low-Sodium Chicken Stock (page 225)

1 tablespoon freshly squeezed lemon juice

¹/₄ teaspoon salt

1 cup uncooked couscous

POACHED HALIBUT

1 tablespoon minced shallots

1 bay leaf

1 sprig thyme

¹/₂ cup white wine

¹/₂ cup water

1 tablespoon freshly squeezed lemon juice

4 boneless and skinless halibut fillets, about 6 ounces each

NUTRITIONAL
INFORMATION PER
SERVING

Total Calories: 385

Total Fat: 6 gm.

Saturated Fat: 1 gm.

Cholesterol: 54 mg.

Sodium: 232 mg.

Fiber Rating: 7 gm.

To prepare the vinaigrette, combine the citrus juices in a small saucepan. Bring to a boil over medium heat and reduce by one-third until about 3 tablespoons remain. Transfer to a mixing bowl and let cool. Whisk in the shallots, chives, and sugar. Slowly whisk in the olive oil until it is completely emulsified. Set aside.

To prepare the couscous, place the stock and lemon juice in a saucepan, season with the salt, and bring to a boil. Stir in the couscous and remove the pan from the heat. Cover with a lid and let stand while preparing the halibut.

Place all the ingredients for the halibut in a saucepan. Cover the pan and cook over medium heat for 3 minutes. Turn the fillets over and continue cooking for 3 to 5 minutes.

Just before serving, fluff the couscous with a fork. Spoon a mound of the couscous in the center of each serving plate and top with the poached halibut. Drizzle each halibut with 1 tablespoon of the vinaigrette.

❧

NOTE: Poaching is a fat-free, quick cooking method for many fish and poultry dishes, and it's a good way to add flavor if you season the poaching liquid with whatever flavors you want the food to absorb.

Pan-Seared Scallops with Tomato Fettuccine, Snow Peas, and Water Chestnuts

I'm a scallop fanatic, which is why I know that Digby, Nova Scotia, is the scallop capital of the world. It may be a small Canadian fishing town, but it is also notable for having one of the highest tides in the world, as measured by the distance between high and low tides. I visited Digby with my family one summer, and we ate scallops at every conceivable opportunity—in soups, on brochettes, with pasta, with vegetable sides, and even in breakfast hash and omelets. The secret to cooking scallops is to sear them in a hot pan over high heat; this technique seals in their juices and gives them a firm, crisp texture. Otherwise, their juices will escape and the scallops will boil in them, diminishing both flavor and texture. These same qualities are accentuated with the outstanding combination of scallops, snow peas, and water chestnuts, which work so well together, while the exotic touch added by the curry powder rounds out the flavors. To cook everything properly, use two separate pans or cook in two batches.

24 sea scallops (about 1 pound), rinsed and patted dry

2 tablespoons minced garlic

1 tablespoon minced shallots

1 cup white wine

32 snow peas

1 cup sliced canned water chestnuts, rinsed and drained

1 tablespoon curry powder

1 cup Low-Sodium Chicken Stock (page 225)

1 pound dried tomato fettucine (or plain fettucine), cooked, drained, and cooled

2 tablespoons freshly squeezed lemon juice

1/4 cup chopped cilantro

1/2 teaspoon salt

Freshly ground black pepper to taste

Heat a nonstick sauté pan lightly coated with nonstick cooking spray. Add 12 of the scallops and sauté over medium-high heat for 1 to $1^{1}/_{2}$ minutes on each side, until browned. Remove from the pan and set aside. Repeat for the remaining scallops.

Using the same pan, add 1 tablespoon of the garlic and $^{1}/_{2}$ tablespoon of the shallots, and sauté over medium-high heat for 30 seconds. Deglaze with $^{1}/_{2}$ cup of the white wine. Stir in half of the snow peas, water chestnuts, curry powder, and stock until thoroughly combined. Add half of the pasta and sautéed scallops, stir gently to combine, and heat through. Stir in half of the lemon juice, cilantro, salt, and pepper. Keep warm. Repeat for the remaining batch.

To serve, place the pasta in each serving bowl, arranging 6 scallops on top of each serving. Arrange the snow peas in between the scallops and serve immediately.

NOTE: Unless you are allergic to them, don't be afraid to eat shellfish. They may have a reputation for containing cholesterol, but remember that you need to be more concerned with your intake of saturated fat. If you enjoy shellfish, include them once a week, and keep the serving size down to 6 ounces or less per person. Considering this is an entrée with a starch component, the level of calories in this recipe is reasonable, especially if you make this the main meal of the day.

NUTRITIONAL
INFORMATION PER
SERVING

Total Calories: 540

Total Fat: 3 gm.

Saturated Fat: 0.4 gm.

Cholesterol: 37 mg.

Sodium: 448 mg.

Fiber Rating: 0.3 mg.

Gulf Shrimp Stir-Fry with Bok Choy, Mushrooms, and a Trio of Peppers

SERVES: 4

This recipe is a cross between Texas Gulf Coast and Asian cuisines. It is an appropriate interplay of ingredients and styles because over the last 25 years or so there has been a big influx of Asian (and especially Vietnamese) immigrants to the Gulf Coast. Many brought with them their expertise in the shrimping industry, setting up their own boats. The cultures now seem to exist together easily, a trend that is also evident in the combining of cuisines. Stir-frying, which helps preserve the nutrients in foods, is a healthful technique. If you own a wok, use it for this recipe.

1 tablespoon canola oil

16 extra-large shrimp (about 1 pound), shelled and deveined

2 tablespoons minced garlic

1 red bell pepper, seeded and diced

1 yellow bell pepper, seeded and diced

1 green bell pepper, seeded and diced

6 large shiitake mushrooms, stemmed and sliced, or 10 button mushrooms, unstemmed and sliced

1 small bok choy, trimmed of outer leaves and chopped

1 cup sliced canned water chestnuts

2 tablespoons low-sodium soy sauce

1 cup Low-Sodium Chicken Stock (page 225)

4 scallions, sliced

1 teaspoon ground ginger

1/4 teaspoon red pepper flakes

2 tablespoons chopped fresh cilantro

2 tablespoons freshly squeezed lemon juice

Heat the canola oil in a large sauté pan. When the pan is hot, add the shrimp and stir-fry over high heat for 2 to 3 minutes, until they just turn pink. Remove from the pan and set aside. Using the same pan, add the garlic, bell peppers, mushrooms, bok choy, and water chestnuts, and stir-fry for 2 to 3 minutes.

Deglaze the pan with the soy sauce and stock and continue cooking until the vegetables are tender and crisp. Stir in the scallions, ginger, pepper flakes, cilantro, lemon juice, and cooked shrimp, and stir-fry until all the liquid has evaporated and the vegetables are lightly glazed. Serve immediately.

NOTE: Japanese soy sauce is lighter in flavor than Chinese soy sauce. It is made from fermented soy beans, wheat, and malt seeds, and a little goes a long way. Because of the strong flavor and high sodium content, you might want to consider diluting soy sauce with water, even the low-sodium variety that contains about half the sodium.

NUTRITIONAL INFORMATION PER SERVING
Total Calories: 180
Total Fat: 5 gm.
Saturated Fat: 1 gm.
Cholesterol: 221 mg.
Sodium: 589 mg.
Fiber Rating: 1 mg.

Grilled Chicken Breast with Melon Salsa and Tortilla and Arugula Salad

*H*ere's another popular summer item from the Rittenhouse menu that contrasts peppery, spicy arugula with fragrant, sweet melons. Arugula, also known as rocket lettuce, is native to the Mediterranean and is widely used in Italian cuisine. Italian neighborhoods, such as South Philly, or Italian markets, are excellent sources of this delicious salad green. The tortilla strips give the dish height and structure, and a crunchiness that contrasts with the soft textures of the other ingredients.

SERVES: 4

MELON SALSA

- 1/2 cup diced cantaloupe melon or crenshaw melon
- 1/2 cup diced honeydew melon
- 1 large fresh jalapeño chile, seeded and thinly sliced (use more or less to taste)
- 2 tablespoons finely diced red onion
- 1 teaspoon chopped fresh cilantro
- 1/2 teaspoon chopped fresh mint
- 1 teaspoon freshly squeezed lime juice

SALAD

- 4 corn tortillas, cut into 1/2-inch-thick strips
- 4 ounces arugula (2 1/4 cups, firmly packed)
- Juice of 2 lemons
- 4 boneless and skinless chicken breasts, about 5 ounces each

Preheat the oven to 325° and prepare the grill.

Thoroughly combine all the salsa ingredients in a mixing bowl and set aside.

To prepare the salad, lightly coat a baking sheet with nonstick cooking spray. Place the tortilla strips on the baking sheet without overlapping and bake in the oven for 20 minutes, or until golden brown. Remove from the oven and let cool.

Place the arugula in a large mixing bowl and toss gently but thoroughly with the lemon juice. Set aside.

Place the chicken breasts on the medium-hot grill and grill for 5 to 8 minutes per side, or until cooked through and tender.

To serve, place some of the arugula salad in a strip down the left-hand side of each serving plate and some of the salsa on the right-hand side of each plate. Slice the chicken breasts and place on top of the arugula salad. Garnish the chicken with the tortilla strips, placing them upright in between each slice. Serve immediately.

❧

NOTE: For an even more colorful presentation, use two blue corn and two yellow corn tortillas, or, even better, try tracking down red tortillas from a gourmet Southwestern food store (if you have one nearby) and using one or two of those as well.

NUTRITIONAL
INFORMATION PER
SERVING

Total Calories: 247

Total Fat: 7 gm.

Saturated Fat: 2 gm.

Cholesterol: 65 mg.

Sodium: 113 mg.

Fiber Rating: 3 gm.

Turkey Fajitas with Peppers and Onions and Summer Vegetable Escabeche

SERVES: 4

*F*ajitas are not Mexican, as many people think, although they are derived from that culinary tradition; they are a fairly recent innovation, and likely originated in the San Antonio, Texas region. The word "fajitas" means "belts," referring to the grilled strips of meat used for the dish. Beef and chicken are the two types most commonly used. In this recipe, the turkey is pan-seared, but you can grill it if you prefer, especially if you prefer a smoky, slightly charred flavor. The escabeche is a great way of using summer vegetables. You can substitute zucchini, green beans, or asparagus for the vegetables in the recipe.

VEGETABLE ESCABECHE

$1/2$ cup white wine vinegar

$3/4$ cup water

$1/4$ teaspoon sugar

$1/4$ teaspoon salt

8 ounces broccoli florets (about 3 cups)

8 ounces cauliflower florets (about 3 cups)

$1/2$ onion, cut into $1/4$-inch-thick slices

1 carrot, peeled and cut into $1/4$-inch-thick slices

1 fresh jalapeño chile, seeded and sliced

1 teaspoon chopped fresh cilantro

1 tablespoon olive oil

Freshly ground black pepper to taste

TURKEY FAJITAS

12 ounces boneless and skinless turkey breast, thinly sliced

2 green bell peppers, seeded and julienned

2 red bell peppers, seeded and julienned

1 onion, thinly sliced

1 fresh jalapeño chile, seeded and thinly sliced

4 tablespoons chopped fresh cilantro

5 limes, cut in half

8 flour tortillas

To prepare the escabeche, place the vinegar, water, sugar, and salt in a saucepan. Bring the mixture to a boil over high heat, stirring occasionally. Remove the pan from the heat and stir in the broccoli, cauliflower, onions, carrots, and jalapeños, and let cool.

When the mixture has cooled, add the cilantro, olive oil, and pepper, and toss together to thoroughly coat. Allow the mixture to marinate for 1 to 2 hours before serving. The escabeche will last up to 3 days in the refrigerator if completely covered by the liquid.

To prepare the fajitas, place a large nonstick sauté pan coated with non-stick cooking spray over high heat. Add the turkey and sear on all sides until brown. Add the bell peppers, onions, and jalapeños and stir-fry for about 5 minutes. Squeeze the juice of 3 of the limes into the mixture and continue to stir-fry for 3 minutes, or until the mixture is cooked through. Stir in the cilantro and remove the pan from the heat. Stir in the juice from the remaining 2 limes and transfer to a serving platter. Keep warm.

Warm the flour tortillas on a hot griddle or in a dry skillet, transfer to a tortilla basket or serving plate, and cover with a kitchen towel to keep warm. Each person can roll the turkey fajitas mixture in the tortillas. Serve with the vegetable escabeche.

❧

NOTE: This is an excellent, filling, low-calorie, high-fiber meal. There are a wealth of antioxidant sources here, and a minimum of sodium contributors. Sour cream is a traditional garnish for fajitas, but you should avoid it for heart-healthy reasons. Fat-free sour cream is now available, or use nonfat plain yogurt instead. Chicken can be used in place of turkey if you prefer.

NUTRITIONAL INFORMATION PER SERVING

Total Calories: 419

Total Fat: 8 gm.

Saturated Fat: 1 gm.

Cholesterol: 70 mg.

Sodium: 212 mg.

Fiber Rating: 7 gm.

Caraway-Crusted Pork Medallions with Vine-Ripened Tomatoes and Red Onions

SERVES: 4

This is a very simple and light dish that I demonstrated at the annual meeting of the Institute of American Culinary Professionals held in Philadelphia in 1996.

It's wonderful that herbs and spices are so flavorful yet so low in calories. The nutty-tasting caraway seeds with their anise tones make a natural partner for pork by enhancing the meat's flavor characteristics. For a finer crust, grind the caraway and dust the pork medallions with it.

12 pork loin medallions, about 2
  ounces each and $1/2$ inch thick

2 tablespoons caraway seeds,
  or to taste

1 tablespoon minced garlic

2 tomatoes, each cut into 8 wedges

2 small red onions, each cut into 8
  wedges

2 tablespoons balsamic vinegar

3 tablespoons julienned fresh basil

Freshly ground black pepper to taste

4 carrots, sliced with a mandolin or
  finely grated, for garnish

4 sprigs oregano, for garnish

Sprinkle the pork medallions on both sides with the caraway seeds. Using your hands, press the seeds onto the meat. Heat a nonstick sauté pan sprayed with nonstick cooking spray. When the pan is hot, add the pork medallions and sear over high heat for 2 to 3 minutes on each side, or until browned and cooked through. Remove from the pan and keep warm.

Using the same pan, add the garlic, tomatoes, and onions and sauté over medium-high heat for 2 to 3 minutes, until the onions are translucent. Deglaze with the vinegar, then add the basil and black pepper and stir well to combine.

Spoon the vegetable mixture at the top of each serving plate. Fan 3 of the pork medallions below and around the vegetables on each plate. Garnish the edge of each plate with a circle of the carrots and garnish the vegetables with the oregano.

NOTE: Pork is becoming known as an acceptable addition to a fat-modified diet, especially as the animals have been deliberately bred much leaner over the years. Even so, the right cut of pork makes all the difference in fat content. For example, 3 ounces of lean pork tenderloin contains 141 calories, 4 grams of fat, 1 gram of saturated fat, and 79 milligrams of cholesterol, while 3 ounces of pork spare ribs contain 338 calories, 26 grams of fat, 10 grams of saturated fat, and 103 milligrams of cholesterol.

NUTRITIONAL
INFORMATION PER
SERVING

Total Calories: 301

Total Fat: 8 gm.

Saturated Fat: 3 gm.

Cholesterol: 158 mg.

Sodium: 120 mg.

Fiber Rating: 1 gm.

Lemongrass-Marinated Filet Mignon Grilled with Oven-Baked Chile Potato Chips

SERVES: 4

*B*eef has certainly made a comeback over the last few years. Even our guests at the Rittenhouse who are conscious of diet and health issues like a little beef now and again. In this recipe, the clean flavors of the marinade—and especially the lemongrass—help to cut the richness of the beef filet. Baked chips are much healthier than fried. The secret to the chips is to slice the potatoes as thinly as possible so they cook quickly and crisply. If you are seeking variety, season the chips with garlic powder or Cajun seasoning instead of the chile powder.

MARINADE

1 stalk fresh lemongrass, minced

1 tablespoon minced garlic

1 scallion, thinly sliced

1 tablespoon coriander seed

1 tablespoon curry powder

1 cup red wine

$^1/_4$ cup water

4 filets mignon, about 5 ounces each, trimmed

CHIPS

2 Idaho potatoes

Pure red chile powder to taste

SAUCE

1 cup Low-Sodium Beef Broth (page 225)

1 tablespoon cornstarch

1 tablespoon water

Combine all the marinade ingredients in a mixing bowl. Add the filets and marinate in the refrigerator for 4 to 6 hours.

Preheat the oven to 350° and prepare the grill.

To make the potato chips, peel and thinly slice the potatoes in a food processor (or by hand), keeping the potato slices immersed in water to prevent them from browning. Drain the potatoes and pat dry. Arrange the potato slices about 1 inch apart on a baking sheet coated with nonstick cooking spray. Bake in the oven for 25 to 30 minutes, or until golden brown. Remove from the oven and let cool slightly, then sprinkle with the chile powder.

Remove the filets from the marinade, reserving the marinade. Grill the filets over medium heat for 8 to 10 minutes until medium-rare, or until cooked to desired doneness.

Meanwhile, to make the sauce, strain the reserved marinade into a saucepan. Add the broth, bring to a boil, and reduce the mixture by half. Mix together the cornstarch and water in a cup and whisk into the reduced liquid. Whisk constantly until the mixture thickens.

To serve, place the filets in the center of each serving plate. Spoon the sauce over each filet and top with the chips.

NOTE: The marinade also works well with pork. You don't have to entirely eliminate beef from your diet if you have a cholesterol problem. Choose lean cuts, keep the portion size to between 3 and 5 ounces, and balance your intake of red meat with a vegetarian dish for the other main meal of the day.

NUTRITIONAL
INFORMATION PER
SERVING

Total Calories: 276

Total Fat: 9 gm.

Saturated Fat: 4 gm.

Cholesterol: 80 mg.

Sodium: 64 mg.

Fiber Rating: 2 gm.

Stir-Fried Tropical Fruit Napoleon with Sesame Seed Meringues

SERVES: 4

Summer and desserts mean tropical fruits, and what better way to present this seasonal bounty than in an elegant napoleon? Dessert napoleons usually involve layers of puff pastry, but here we use crispy, nonfat meringue wafers, allowing the flavors of the fruits and sesame oil supply the requisite richness. I find mangoes and papayas to be the most refreshing of fruit—nothing beats off the heat better—but you can substitute stone fruit such as peaches, plums, apricots, nectarines, or poached pears. When buying mangoes, test for ripeness by feel (they should be slightly tender to the touch) and by smell (they should exude a floral, perfumed aroma). Impress a dinner party with an napoleon dinner: Begin with the Beefsteak Tomato and Vidalia Onion Napoleon (Spring), followed by the Oven-Roasted Beefsteak Tomato, Spinach, and Zucchini Napoleon (Summer), and finish up with this recipe.

MERINGUES

2 egg whites

³/₄ cup sugar

2 tablespoons sesame seeds, lightly
    toasted

TROPICAL FRUIT

²/₃ cup freshly squeezed orange juice

1 banana, peeled and thickly sliced

1 kiwifruit, peeled and cubed

¹/₂ tablespoon sesame oil

¹/₂ tablespoon sunflower oil

¹/₂ tablespoon peeled and grated
    fresh ginger

1 vanilla bean, split in half lengthwise
    and seeds scraped

1 mango, peeled, pitted, and cubed

¹/₂ papaya, peeled, seeded, and cubed

4 large sprigs mint, for garnish

Preheat the oven to 200°.

To prepare the meringues, add the egg whites and sugar to a mixing bowl and place over a hot water bath (bain marie) or a pan of hot water for 2 minutes to warm through. Remove the bowl and beat with a heavy-duty mixer on high speed until stiff. Drop large spoonfuls of the meringue onto a non-stick baking sheet (there should be enough mixture for 12 meringues; use 2 sheets if necessary). Using a spatula, spread each meringue into a 3-inch circle and sprinkle the sesame seeds on top. Transfer to the oven and bake for 1 1/2 hours.

For the fruit, combine the orange juice, banana, and kiwifruit in a small mixing bowl and marinate for 10 minutes. Heat the sesame and sunflower oils in a wok or large sauté pan. Add the ginger and vanilla bean seeds and pod to the hot pan and cook over medium heat for 1 to 2 minutes, until aromatic. Stir in the mango and papaya, and cook for 2 to 3 minutes over medium-high heat until lightly browned. Strain the banana and kiwifruit, reserving the orange juice, and add the fruit, gently stir-frying for about 1 minute. Stir in half of the reserved orange juice and reduce until almost dry. Add the remaining orange juice and gently stir-fry for 1 minute longer. Remove from the heat, remove the vanilla bean, and set aside.

To assemble the dessert, place 1 meringue in the center of each serving plate. Place 1 rounded tablespoon of the fruit mixture on top of each meringue and top with another meringue. Spoon another rounded tablespoon of the fruit mixture on top of the last meringue and top with a third meringue. Drizzle each napoleon with the fruit cooking liquid. Garnish with the mint and serve.

NUTRITIONAL
INFORMATION PER
SERVING

Total Calories: 296

Total Fat: 6 gm.

Saturated Fat: 1 gm.

Cholesterol: 0 mg.

Sodium: 31 mg.

Fiber Rating: 4 gm.

Black Plum and Sour Cream Tart with Oatmeal Streusel

*T*here are countless varieties of plums, ranging in color from yellow to red, green, and blue, but my favorites are the sweet and lusciously juicy black plums. Their softness combines well in this recipe with the crispy texture of the oats in the streusel topping ("streusel" is the German word for sprinkle). This recipe owes much to the versatility of nonfat dairy substitutes and their ability to simulate rich, custardlike cream fillings. Custards come in all types and styles, and because of the egg whites they contain, they should be cooked slowly to develop a smooth consistency.

SERVES: 6

TART SHELL

$^3/_4$ cup nonfat graham cracker crumbs

$1^1/_2$ tablespoons fat-free vegetable oil spread, melted

FILLING

4 fresh black plums, pitted and cut into 6 wedges each

$^3/_4$ cup nonfat sour cream

$^1/_4$ cup sugar

$^1/_2$ cup egg substitute (such as Eggbeaters)

$^1/_4$ teaspoon ground coriander

STREUSEL TOPPING

$^1/_3$ cup quick oats

1 tablespoon sugar

$^1/_3$ cup all-purpose flour

$^1/_4$ cup fat-free vegetable oil spread

NUTRITIONAL
INFORMATION PER
SERVING

Total Calories: 222

Total Fat: 2 gm.

Saturated Fat: 0.3 gm.

Cholesterol: 0.2 mg.

Sodium: 288 mg.

Fiber Rating: 2 gm.

Preheat the oven to 325°.

To prepare the tart shell, mix together the graham cracker crumbs and melted vegetable oil spread in a mixing bowl. Press the mixture onto the bottom and sides of an 8-inch spring-form pan.

To prepare the filling, arrange the plum wedges to cover the bottom of the tart shell. With a heavy duty electric mixer on low speed, beat the sour cream, sugar, egg substitute, and coriander in a mixing bowl until smooth. Pour the mixture over the plums and set aside.

To prepare the topping, place all the ingredients in a mixing bowl. Using your hands, mix together until crumbly. Sprinkle the mixture over the filling. Transfer the tart to the oven and bake for 35 minutes, or until the filling has set. Remove from the oven and let cool slightly before cutting.

NOTE: Nonfat graham cracker crumbs are available at most health food stores and many supermarkets. By serving 8 instead of 6, this tart will contain only 167 calories per serving.

Phyllo Basket with Lemongrass Sherbet and Raspberry-Peach Compote

Here's an unusual dessert that features lemongrass, a versatile ingredient. It's the herb of choice in Thai cuisine, where it is usually incorporated into soups and sauces to help emphasize surrounding flavors while adding its own burst of refreshing, citrus-like oils. Sherbets are basically the same as sorbets, except that unlike sorbets they can contain milk, as in this recipe. Like ice cream, they are both very easy—and fun—to make at home, requiring only a small investment in an ice-cream machine. The mild acidity of the raspberries and peaches in the compote provides an abundance of fruit flavors without making the dessert overly sweet. If you'd like to give this dessert an even more Asian touch, you can add $^1/_2$ teaspoon of minced fresh ginger to the sherbet ingredients.

SERVES: 4

SHERBET

2 cups water

1 stalk fresh lemongrass

$^3/_4$ cup nonfat milk

$^1/_2$ cup sugar

$^1/_2$ vanilla bean, split in half lengthwise
   and seeds scraped

PHYLLO BASKETS

4 sheets phyllo dough

$1^1/_2$ tablespoons fat-free vegetable
   spread, melted

$1^1/_2$ teaspoons sugar

1 teaspoon ground caraway seed

COMPOTE

$^1/_4$ cup white wine

2 tablespoons all-fruit peach
   preserves

2 fresh peaches, peeled, pitted,
   and thinly sliced ($^1/_4$- to $^1/_8$-inch
   thick slices)

$^1/_2$ cup fresh raspberries

To prepare the sherbet, place the water and lemongrass in a saucepan. Bring to a boil over high heat and reduce by half. Turn down the heat to low and stir in the milk, sugar, and the vanilla seeds and pod. Cook for 10 minutes. Strain through a fine-mesh strainer and pour into the tub of an ice cream maker. Freeze according to the manufacturer's directions.

Preheat the oven to 350°.

Lay out the phyllo dough on a work surface. Brush each sheet with the melted vegetable spread and sprinkle with the sugar and caraway seeds. Cut each sheet into quarters to form 4 equal squares and line 4 large cups of a nonstick muffin tin with the phyllo, creating a basket shape. Transfer to the oven and bake for 12 minutes, or until golden brown.

To prepare the compote, combine the wine and preserves in a saucepan and bring to a simmer. Stir in the peaches and cook for 3 to 5 minutes, until tender. Remove from the heat and stir in the raspberries. Rewarm before serving, if necessary.

To assemble the dessert, place a phyllo basket in the center of each serving plate. Place a scoop of the sherbet in each basket. Spoon the warm compote on top of the sherbet and serve immediately.

NOTE: For the caraway in this recipe, like all seeds and spices that need to be ground, it's best to buy them whole and then grind them yourself in a spice mill or small coffee grinder reserved for the purpose.

All-fruit preserves are often better-tasting than those made with sugar because the flavor of the fruit is so intense. They still contain calories (8 to 16 per teaspoon) because of the fruit's natural sugars. Make your own by simply cooking fresh fruit down to its concentrated form.

NUTRITIONAL
INFORMATION PER
SERVING

Total Calories: 230

Total Fat: 1 gm.

Saturated Fat: 0 gm.

Cholesterol: 81 mg.

Sodium: 67 mg.

Fiber Rating: 3 gm.

Blueberry and Port Cobbler with Sweet Potato Dumpling Crust

*B*erry cobblers are a traditional Southern dessert distinguished by their biscuit-like crust topped with a sprinkling of sugar. Cobbler crusts made with sweet potatoes also have a long and illustrious Southern heritage—a recipe is included in the Picayune Cookbook, *which dates back to the 1830s. You can substitute blackberries or raspberries for the blueberries if you wish.*

SERVES: 6

CRUST

1/2 cup cake or pastry flour

1 tablespoon sugar

1 tablespoon baking powder

1/4 cup fat-free vegetable oil spread (margarine)

1/2 cup sweet potato purée (about 1 medium sweet potato)

1/4 teaspoon pure vanilla extract

3/4 cup nonfat sour cream

FILLING

3 cups fresh blueberries

1 tablespoon all-purpose flour

1 1/2 tablespoons sugar

1/2 cup port

Superfine sugar, for dusting (optional)

NUTRITIONAL INFORMATION PER SERVING

Total Calories: 170

Total Fat: 1 gm.

Saturated Fat: 0 gm.

Cholesterol: 0 mg.

Sodium: 256 mg.

Fiber Rating: 3 gm.

To prepare the crust, sift together the flour, sugar, and baking powder into a mixing bowl. Mix in the vegetable oil spread and sweet potato purée until just combined and a firm mass forms. Add the vanilla and sour cream and work the dough together briefly with your hands until thoroughly combined. Refrigerate for 1 hour.

Preheat the oven to 350°. To prepare the filling, thoroughly mix the blueberries, flour, sugar, and port in a large casserole dish. Top evenly with the crust mixture and transfer to the oven. Bake for 35 minutes, or until golden brown. Serve the cobbler warm, with a sprinkling of superfine sugar, if desired.

Fall

APPETIZERS

Ginger Pumpkin Soup with Shiitake Mushrooms / 102

Lobster and Asparagus Risotto / 104

Smoked Trout and Fennel Ravioli with White Bean and Sage Compote / 106

Mushroom and Low-Fat Ricotta Phyllo Cannelloni with a Roasted Tomato Coulis / 109

SALADS

Watercress and Bibb Salad with Jicama and Toasted Pumpkin Seed Vinaigrette / 112

Yolk-Free Caesar Salad with Roasted-Pepper Pesto Croutons / 113

Fresh Spinach and Poached Pear Salad with Hearts of Palm and Port Vinaigrette / 115

Warm Cucumber and Smoked Salmon Salad with Five Grain Croutons / 118

ENTRÉES

Ten-Vegetable Fried Brown Rice / 120

Sautéed Sea Scallops with Autumn Vegetable Couscous / 122

Poached Orange Roughy with Rhubarb and Riesling Sauce / 124

Apple Cider-Poached Chicken with Black Currant Barley / 126

Chicken and Lobster Ballottine with Melted Leeks and Sundried Tomato Broth / 128

Braised Lamb Shank Pot au Feu / 132

Roasted Lamb Loin with Fresh Sauerkraut / 134

Apricot-Stuffed Loin of Pork / 137

Pan-Seared New York Strip with Texas Bean Ragout / 139

DESSERTS

Butternut Cheesecake with Poached Cranberries and Lime Zest / 141

Black Forest Crepes with Cocoa Sorbet / 143

Gratin of Apple and Mapled Citrus / 145

Poached Asian Pears with Lemon-, Ginger-, and Anise-Flavored Fruit Compote / 148

Opposite: Sautéed Sea Scallops with Autumn Vegetable Couscous, page 122.

Ginger Pumpkin Soup with Shiitake Mushrooms

SERVES: 8

This recipe is about as autumnal as it gets. I like to get my kids involved around Halloween and the holiday season, carving pumpkins and helping with pumpkin pie and easy dishes, like this soup. This recipe can be doubled, so if you'd like to use a larger, three-pound pumpkin, you'll find this soup ideal for Thanksgiving entertaining or for freezing. The buttermilk and ginger counteract the richness of the pumpkin, while the shiitakes add a pleasantly deep, woodsy flavor. For extra effect, serve the soup in small carved-out pumpkins.

1 small pumpkin, about $1^1/_2$ pounds, unpeeled, cut in quarters, seeded, and inner fibers removed

$1^1/_2$ quarts Low-Sodium Chicken Stock (page 225)

1 tablespoon minced garlic

$^1/_2$ teaspoon finely minced fresh ginger

1 teaspoon ground ginger

1 cup nonfat buttermilk

$^1/_4$ cup honey

Juice of 1 freshly squeezed lemon

Pinch of ground allspice

Freshly ground black pepper to taste

12 shiitake mushrooms, stemmed and sliced $^1/_4$ inch thick

2 fresh basil leaves, thinly sliced, for garnish

Preheat the oven to 350°.

Place the pumpkin on a baking sheet skin side down and bake in the oven for 30 minutes. Remove from the oven and let cool slightly. Peel the skin from the flesh and discard the skin. Cut the pumpkin into 2-inch squares.

Combine the pumpkin with $^1/_2$ cup of the stock, the garlic, and ginger in a large saucepan and sweat over low heat for 10 minutes. Add the remaining stock, increase the heat, and bring the mixture to a boil. Reduce the heat and lightly simmer the soup for 30 minutes, until the pumpkin is tender. Stir in the ground ginger, buttermilk, honey, lemon juice, allspice, and black pepper.

Transfer the soup to a blender or food processor and purée until smooth. Transfer back to a clean saucepan, stir in the mushrooms, and return to a simmer. Cook the soup for 2 minutes. Ladle the soup into serving bowls and garnish with the basil.

❧

NOTE: Don't be fooled by its name—buttermilk is made from nonfat milk and a small amount of added butterfat that gives it a nutritional profile similar to 1% milk. However, buttermilk is higher in sodium. Buttermilk contains substantially less fat than whole milk. You can substitute nonfat milk for the buttermilk in this recipe if you prefer.

NUTRITIONAL
INFORMATION PER
SERVING

Total Calories: 78

Total Fat: 0.4 gm.

Saturated Fat: 0

Cholesterol: 1 mg.

Sodium: 35 mg.

Fiber Rating: 1 gm

Lobster and Asparagus Risotto

SERVES: 4

The very first risotto I ever ate was at a restaurant in New York, and yes, it contained lobster. I tasted it and fell in love. Risotto is perfect for fall because of its hearty nature, and because fall is peak season for both lobster and California asparagus, this dish is a perfect match. Risotto is a very adaptable and flexible medium; you can substitute tomato juice or even pineapple juice for the chicken stock, and play with the combinations of flavors of the other ingredients. Some people are intimidated by risotto, as it has a reputation for having to be cooked just right, but it's not as hard to cook as most people think. In this recipe, for example, you don't even have to stand over it—you finish it in the oven until the liquid has evaporated. The recipe for this appetizer can easily be doubled for a filling entrée for four.

6 ounces lobster tail meat (about 1 or 2 tails), cut into $1/8$-inch-thick pieces

1 tablespoon minced garlic

2 tablespoons minced shallots

1 red bell pepper, seeded and diced

6 tablespoons white wine

2 cups Arborio rice

3 tablespoons freshly squeezed lemon juice

4 cups Low-Sodium Chicken Stock (page 225)

1 large tomato, blanched, peeled, seeded, and diced

12 asparagus spears, cut in half on the diagonal

$1^{1}/_{2}$ tablespoons chopped fresh dill

$1^{1}/_{2}$ tablespoons thinly sliced fresh basil

1 teaspoon salt

4 sprigs dill, for garnish

Preheat the oven to 400°.

Coat a high-sided, ovenproof sauté pan or skillet with nonstick cooking spray and place over medium-high heat. Add the lobster, garlic, shallots, and red bell pepper, and sauté for $1^1/_2$ minutes, or until the lobster is just cooked. Remove the lobster from the pan and set aside to cool.

Add the wine, rice, and lemon juice to the pan, stir together thoroughly, and cook for 2 minutes. Add 1 cup of the stock and continue cooking, stirring constantly, until the liquid has just evaporated. Add $1^1/_2$ cups more of the stock, and, stirring constantly, allow the stock to evaporate again.

Stir in the remaining $1^1/_2$ cups of the stock, the diced tomato, asparagus, dill, basil, and salt. Transfer the pan to the oven and finish cooking for about 20 minutes, until all of the liquid has evaporated. Remove the pan from the oven and stir in the reserved lobster.

Spoon the risotto onto the serving plates, arranging the lobster meat on top of the rice. Garnish with the dill sprigs and serve.

❧

NOTE: Shellfish used to be considered taboo for a cholesterol- and fat-modified diet because they have substantial amounts of cholesterol. However, we now know that it is the saturated fat in foods that we need to be concerned about, and the fat in fish and shellfish, unlike that found in meat, is largely from polyunsaturated sources. Therefore, consuming 3 or 4 ounces of lobster, shrimp, or crab at least two or three times a week should not be a concern.

NUTRITIONAL
INFORMATION PER
SERVING

Total Calories: 424

Total Fat: 1 gm.

Saturated Fat: 0.3 gm.

Cholesterol: 30 mg.

Sodium: 706 mg.

Fiber Rating: 2 gm.

Smoked Trout and Fennel Ravioli with White Bean and Sage Compote

SERVES: 4

This is a dish of rustic flavors, offset by the elegant tones of the aromatic fennel. Smoked fish contrasts well with the richness of beans, and because trout have firm texture and a relatively high level of natural oils, they take to smoking very well. The same is true of salmon, to which trout is related. There's something very special about catching trout in a fast-flowing stream or river, or from a boat on a lake, and then frying it up later over a campfire. You just can't beat it—the freshness and flavor are unique. Unfortunately, farmed trout don't have the same delicious nuances of taste.

COMPOTE

1 cup dried white navy beans, rinsed and soaked overnight

2 quarts cold water

1 tablespoon olive oil

1 tablespoon minced garlic

1 cup Low-Sodium Chicken Stock (page 225)

1 tablespoon minced fresh sage

1^1/$_2$ teaspoons sliced fresh chives

RAVIOLI FILLING

1 fennel bulb (about 6 ounces)

4 ounces skinless smoked trout

1 tablespoon chopped garlic

Juice of 1 freshly squeezed lemon

^{1}/$_2$ tablespoon minced fresh chives

RAVIOLI

1^1/$_4$ cups semolina flour

1 cup all-purpose flour

^{1}/$_4$ teaspoon salt

3 egg whites

2 tablespoons water

1 egg white, beaten

2 quarts water

Preheat the oven to 400°.

To prepare the compote, drain and rinse the beans and place in a saucepan. Add the water (or enough to cover the beans by 1 inch), and bring to a boil over high heat. Reduce the heat to a simmer and cook for 35 minutes, or until just tender. Drain the beans and let cool.

Meanwhile, heat the olive oil in a sauté pan. Add the cooked beans and the garlic and sauté over medium heat for 1 to 2 minutes. Add the stock and reduce until the liquid has just evaporated. Remove the pan from the heat, stir in the minced sage and chives, and reserve.

To prepare the filling, wrap the fennel bulb in aluminum foil, place on a baking sheet, and bake in the oven for 30 minutes, or until soft. Remove from the oven and let cool. Coarsely chop the fennel and place in a blender together with the smoked trout and garlic. Blend until smooth. Transfer to a mixing bowl and fold in the lemon juice and minced chives. Keep refrigerated.

To prepare the pasta, combine the flours and salt in a mixing bowl. Transfer to a pasta board or wooden work surface and make a well in the center. Place the 3 egg whites and the water in the well and, using a fork or scraper, fold the flour in from the inner rim of the well. Add the remaining flour, working outwards, and then knead the dough with your hands until it forms a ball. Using the palms of your hands, continue to knead by pushing the dough away from you on the work surface for 3 to 5 minutes, until it becomes firm, tough, and hard to knead. Place the dough in a bowl and cover with a damp towel or plastic wrap. Let sit for at least 30 minutes in a cool place or in the refrigerator.

NUTRITIONAL
INFORMATION PER
SERVING

Total Calories: 434

Total Fat: 5 gm.

Saturated Fat: 1 gm.

Cholesterol: 20 mg.

Sodium: 447 mg.

Fiber Rating: 2 gm.

Flatten the dough out with your hands and then roll to a thickness of $1/16$ inch or less; if using a pasta machine, use a setting of 3 or 2. Using a 4-inch round cutter, cut out 12 circles of pasta. Brush the egg wash in a $1/2$-inch strip along the edge of each pasta round. Place 1 tablespoon of the reserved filling on each round and fold over in a half-moon shape. Using your fingers, gently seal, removing all the air from each ravioli.

Bring the water to a boil in a saucepan. Place the ravioli in the water and boil for 5 minutes or until al dente. Drain, place 3 ravioli on each serving plate, and serve with the compote.

NOTE: Sage works very well with starches of all kinds. It's especially good in poultry stuffings and mixed in with polenta. The semolina flour used to make the ravioli is made from high-gluten durum wheat.

Mushroom and Lowfat Ricotta Phyllo Cannelloni with Roasted Tomato Coulis

*W*ild mushrooms are a sure-fire harbinger of fall, and they seem to complement just about every dish of the season. The thin, papery, strudel-like phyllo dough is fun to work with. I first used phyllo dough when I studied with Madeleine Kamman; she made it by hand, which requires unbelievable skill, and I've never seen anyone do it since. Phyllo is very versatile—it is used in many cuisines, from its native Greece and Turkey to contemporary French, modern Southwestern, and Pacific Rim cuisines. Here I use phyllo instead of the traditional cannelloni pasta. Its crispness contrasts with the soft ricotta and the meaty mushrooms, making an intriguing combination. I think this dish proves that the Italian influence of South Philly is finally catching up to me!

SERVES: 4

FILLING

1 tablespoon olive oil

10 ounces assorted mushrooms (such as shiitake, oyster, chanterelle, and button), finely diced

1 tablespoon minced garlic

1 tablespoon minced shallots

$^1/_2$ cup lowfat ricotta cheese

2 tablespoons minced fresh basil

Freshly cracked black pepper to taste

SAUCE

1 teaspoon olive oil

6 plum tomatoes, cut in quarters

$^1/_2$ onion, diced

1 tablespoon minced garlic

$1^1/_2$ cups Low-Sodium Chicken Stock (page 225)

1 tablespoon chopped fresh basil

4 sheets phyllo dough

12 small shiitake mushrooms, for garnish

4 sprigs of mâche or watercress, for garnish

To prepare the filling, heat the olive oil in a sauté pan. Add the mushrooms and sauté over medium heat for 2 to 3 minutes. Add the garlic and shallots and sauté for 2 to 3 minutes more. Remove the pan from the heat and stir in the cheese, basil, and black pepper. Keep warm.

To prepare the sauce, heat the olive oil in a saucepan. Add the tomatoes and onions and cook over high heat for 5 to 7 minutes. Add the garlic and stock and continue cooking for 8 to 10 minutes, until the tomatoes are tender. Remove from the heat, transfer to a blender or food processor, and purée until smooth. Return to a clean saucepan and stir in the chopped basil. Set aside.

Preheat the oven to 375°.

Lay out a sheet of the phyllo dough on a work surface and lightly brush with water. Top with another phyllo sheet, brush with water, and repeat for the remaining phyllo sheets, stacking them as you go. Cut the stacked phyllo into 2 lengthwise strips. Spread the filling lengthwise on each piece of phyllo and roll into cylinders with the diameter of a half-dollar, in the shape of cannelloni.

Place the phyllo cannelloni on a nonstick baking sheet and bake in the oven for 6 to 8 minutes, or until golden brown. Remove the baking sheet from the oven. Meanwhile, spray a nonstick sauté pan with nonstick cooking spray and set over medium-high heat. Sauté the shiitake mushrooms for 2 to 3 minutes, until wilted. Remove the mushrooms and set aside.

Cut each phyllo cannelloni in half. Neatly trim each end and then cut each half into three pieces; each piece should have one flat end and one diagonal end. Each piece should be a different length (you will have a triangular piece left over, which you will not serve.) Ladle about $^1/_4$ cup of the sauce in the center of each serving plate and stand 3 pieces of cannelloni on the sauce. Garnish the plate with the sautéed mushrooms and the mâche.

NOTE: Ricotta is available in whole milk, lowfat, and skim (fat-free). The skim tends to have a grainy texture, so for a smoother consistency, use lowfat.

NUTRITIONAL
INFORMATION PER
SERVING

Total Calories: 157

Total Fat: 6 gm.

Saturated Fat: 2 gm.

Cholesterol: 89 mg.

Sodium: 50 mg.

Fiber Rating: 2 gm.

Watercress and Bibb Salad with Jicama and Toasted Pumpkin Seed Vinaigrette

SERVES: 4

Peppery watercress and Bibb lettuce are two greens that work well together. Watercress, a member of the mustard family, provides a zippy contrast to the buttery, sweet Bibb; you can substitute mustard greens or arugula for the watercress. Jicama has a crisp, watery, refreshing texture, similar to water chestnuts (which you can substitute if you'd like to add an Asian twist to this salad), and a slightly nutty flavor.

NUTRITIONAL INFORMATION PER SERVING

Total Calories: 91

Total Fat: 8 gm.

Saturated Fat: 1 gm.

Cholesterol: 0 mg.

Sodium: 56 mg.

Fiber Rating: 3 gm.

VINAIGRETTE

1 teaspoon minced garlic

1 teaspoon minced shallots

2 tablespoons canola oil

2 tablespoons Champagne vinegar

2 tablespoons Low-Sodium Chicken Stock (page 225)

SALAD

8 ounces (about 2 heads or 4 cups) Bibb lettuce

4 ounces watercress, leaves only (about 1^1/$_2$ cups, firmly packed)

8 ounces jicama, peeled and julienned (about 1^1/$_2$ cups)

2 tablespoons toasted pumpkin seeds (page 231)

Whisk all the vinaigrette ingredients in a mixing bowl and set aside.

For the salad, arrange the Bibb lettuce on each salad plate. Toss the watercress with the vinaigrette and arrange on top of the Bibb lettuce. Arrange the jicama over the salad and sprinkle each salad with the pumpkin seeds.

NOTE: Jicama is a great source of vitamin C and is low in calories. One cup of jicama contains just 49 calories.

Yolk-Free Caesar Salad with Roasted Pepper-Pesto Croutons

This is another item from the Rittenhouse menu that our guests find hard to believe is heart-healthy. Many diners have remarked that unless they were told or knew in advance there was not yolk in the salad, they wouldn't have known the difference. The Caesar salad was created in 1926 by Alex-Caesar Cardini at his restaurant in Tijuana, and for years it was regarded as a rather exclusive gourmet item. It has become so popular that these days it's not only on the menus in many upscale restaurants, but it's also available in more modest and even fast-food eateries. This version is more colorful than the traditional Caesar, with the roasted red bell pepper croutons contrasting dramatically against the salad greenery.

SERVES: 8

DRESSING

4 egg whites

1 tablespoon Dijon mustard

1 anchovy, coarsely chopped

Juice of 1 freshly squeezed lemon

1 tablespoon grated Parmesan cheese

1/2 cup canola oil

CROUTONS

1 French baguette roll, cut into
    8 slices, 1/4-inch thick

1 red bell pepper, roasted, peeled,
    and seeded (page 231)

1 tablespoon minced garlic

1 tablespoon chopped fresh basil

1 tablespoon chopped fresh thyme

SALAD

1 head romaine lettuce, cut into
    1-inch pieces

Preheat the oven to 375°.

To prepare the dressing, place the egg whites, mustard, anchovy, lemon juice, and cheese in a blender or food processor and blend for 2 minutes, until smooth. Slowly add the oil and blend until emulsified. Set aside.

To prepare the croutons, place the baguette slices on a baking sheet and bake in the oven for 5 minutes, or until golden brown. Remove from the oven. Combine the roasted bell pepper, garlic, basil, and thyme in a food processor and blend until smooth. Spread the bell pepper mixture on the baguette slices and set aside.

Toss the lettuce with $^1/_2$ cup of the dressing in a mixing bowl. Arrange the tossed lettuce on serving plates and garnish with the croutons.

NOTE: If you are especially fond of anchovies and are not concerned about sodium levels, add 1 or 2 more to the dressing.

NUTRITIONAL
INFORMATION PER
SERVING

Total Calories: 103

Total Fat: 6 gm.

Saturated Fat: 1 gm.

Cholesterol: 0.4 mg.

Sodium: 116 mg.

Fiber Rating: 2 gm.

Fresh Spinach and Poached Pear Salad with Hearts of Palm and Port Vinaigrette

Pears and spinach go surprisingly well together. Likewise, spinach and hearts of palm are excellent partners, so these three ingredients make a happy ménage à trois. The vinaigrette goes supremely well with most salads. The secret to its success lies in the quality of port you use—it really does make a difference, so don't stint.

SERVES: 4

POACHED PEARS

2 cups water

¼ cup sugar

2 cups red wine

4 pears, such as Anjou or Bartlett, peeled and cored

SALAD

4 ounces hearts of palm, sliced on the diagonal ¼-inch-thick

4 ounces fresh baby spinach, stems removed (about 3 cups, firmly packed)

VINAIGRETTE

1 cup port, such as Sandeman's or Warre's

2 tablespoons red wine vinegar

1 tablespoon Dijon mustard

1 tablespoon minced garlic

1 tablespoon minced shallots

¼ cup Low-Sodium Chicken Stock (page 225)

Pinch of freshly ground white pepper

To prepare the pears, combine the water, sugar, and red wine in a saucepan and bring to a boil. Add the pears and poach for 15 minutes, or until tender. Remove from the water with a slotted spoon and let cool.

To prepare the vinaigrette, place the port in a small saucepan and reduce to $^1/_4$ cup. Remove from the heat and refrigerate until chilled.

Whisk together the vinegar, mustard, garlic, shallots, stock, and pepper in a mixing bowl. Slowly whisk in the cold port until emulsified. Set aside.

Shingle the spinach leaves and hearts of palm across the top of each serving plate. Place the poached pears at the bottom of each plate (at the 6 o'clock position). Ladle the vinaigrette around the pears, in a pool. Serve immediately.

NOTES: Hearts of palm are the delicate interior tissues of a type of tropical palm tree, usually the cabbage palmetto. If you can find fresh hearts of palm, use them; they have much less sodium than the canned variety and they have a delicious flavor. They are available in many Latin American markets and health foods stores.

If the pears are not quite ripe enough, you can speed up the process by placing them, along with a ripe apple, in a brown paper bag perforated with a few airholes. The apple releases ethylene gas, which stimulates the ripening process.

NUTRITIONAL
INFORMATION PER
SERVING

Total Calories: 172

Total Fat: 1 gm.

Saturated Fat: 0 gm.

Cholesterol: 0 mg.

Sodium: 102 mg.

Fiber Rating: 6 gm.

Warm Cucumber and Smoked Salmon Salad with Five-Grain Croutons

Every year, The Eisenhower Exchange Fellowship Board Meeting is held in Philadelphia—a high-powered event at which statesmen (including most of the living past presidents) and experts in their field advise corporate representatives about business and foreign affairs. In 1993, former President George Bush attended the meeting; when he dined with us at the Rittenhouse, he ordered this salad—and told me he loved it. He even asked for it when he came again the following year. Cucumber, salmon, and red onions are naturally compatible pairings, and the croutons add an appealingly grainy texture to offset the other ingredients. I prefer to use the English (hothouse) cucumbers, which are meatier, more flavorful, and less seedy than regular cucumbers.

SALAD

1 teaspoon olive oil

1 English or hothouse seedless cucumber (about 12 ounces), peeled, seeded, and julienned

1/2 small red onion, julienned

1 1/2 tablespoons unseasoned rice wine vinegar

2 tablespoons Low-Sodium Chicken Stock (page 225)

Freshly ground white pepper to taste

1 tablespoon chopped fresh dill

12 slices thinly sliced smoked salmon (about 6 ounces)

4 sprigs dill, for garnish

CROUTONS

2 (1/4-inch-thick) slices hearty 5-grain loaf

To prepare the croutons, trim the crust from the slices and cut in half. Cut each half diagonally to form 2 triangles (giving you a total of 8 triangles). Toast the triangles lightly on each side under the broiler. Set aside.

To prepare the salad, heat the olive oil in a sauté pan. Add the cucumbers to the hot pan and sauté over high heat for 2 to 3 minutes, stirring constantly to avoid burning. Add the onions and continue sautéing the cucumbers and onions for 2 to 3 minutes longer, or until translucent. Add the vinegar and stock and continue cooking until almost all of the liquid has evaporated. Remove from the heat and stir in the pepper and dill. Set aside

Roll the salmon slices into cylinders and arrange 3 on each plate positioned at 4 o'clock, 6 o'clock, and 8 o'clock. Spoon a mound of the cucumber salad at the top of each plate. Garnish with the dill and arrange 2 croutons on the sides of each plate.

NUTRITIONAL INFORMATION PER SERVING

Total Calories: 104

Total Fat: 3 gm.

Saturated Fat: 1 gm.

Cholesterol: 10 mg.

Sodium: 385 mg.

Fiber Rating: 2 gm.

Ten-Vegetable Fried Brown Rice

SERVES: 4

This dish is one of our most popular lunch items at the Rittenhouse. For a change we sometimes use Arborio rice instead of brown rice, and serve the same dish as a risotto. This Chinese-influenced recipe is very flexible, which makes it fun to cook. For example, you can use green beans instead of asparagus; regular mushrooms or shiitakes instead of straw mushrooms; snap peas instead of snow peas; or you can add some diced parsnip. Straw mushrooms are the rounded, dome-shaped mushroom with a trimmed stem that lend a distinctively earthy flavor and are used extensively in Chinese cooking. They are so-named because they grow on harvested rice paddy straw. Straw mushrooms are available canned, but use fresh mushrooms in this recipe. The fresh pineapple gives this dish an interesting, exotic twist, and it brings all of the other ingredients together.

$^1/_2$ cup uncooked brown rice

$2^1/_2$ cups Low-Sodium Chicken Stock
 (page 225)

1 tablespoon minced garlic

1 $^1/_2$ tablespoons minced fresh ginger

$^1/_2$ cup finely diced red onion

$^1/_3$ cup diced and peeled carrot

$^1/_3$ cup finely diced red bell pepper

$^1/_2$ cup small broccoli florets

$^1/_2$ cup sliced straw mushrooms or
 shiitakes

$^1/_3$ cup snow peas, finely diced

$^1/_3$ cup peas (fresh or frozen)

$^1/_2$ cup diced fresh pineapple

$^1/_3$ cup diced yellow squash

$^1/_3$ cup asparagus tips, cut into
 $^1/_2$-inch slices

$^1/_3$ cup chopped scallions

3 tablespoons chopped cilantro

Pinch of freshly ground white pepper

Place the rice and stock in a saucepan and bring to a boil. Reduce the heat and simmer, covered, for 30 minutes or until all the liquid has been absorbed. Set aside.

In a wok sprayed with nonstick cooking spray, or in a large nonstick pan, sauté the garlic and ginger over medium heat for 1 or 2 minutes, until soft. Add the onions and carrots and stir-fry for 2 minutes. Add the bell peppers, broccoli, and mushrooms, and stir-fry for 1 minute longer. Add the snow peas, green peas, pineapple, squash, and asparagus, and stir-fry for another 2 to 3 minutes. Add the cooked rice, scallions, cilantro, and white pepper, and stir-fry for 2 minutes, or until everything is well combined. Serve immediately.

❧

NOTE: For a spicier version, add some seeded and minced hot fresh Thai (or serrano) chiles.

NUTRITIONAL INFORMATION PER SERVING

Total Calories: 138

Total Fat: 1.0 gm.

Saturated Fat: 0.2 gm.

Cholesterol: 0 mg.

Sodium: 15.5 mg.

Fiber Rating: 3 gm.

Sautéed Sea Scallops with Autumn Vegetable Couscous

SERVES: 4

This is a dish of delicate textures and contrasting colors, and it provides a wonderful opportunity to use autumn squash such as acorn, butternut, or pumpkin—in fact, the more types you use, the better. I prefer the firm texture of the larger sea scallops, but many like the more delicate small bay scallops. Buy scallops that appear translucent and smell fresh; avoid any that look watery or are bright white in color as these are both signs that they have been soaked to increase their weight, which will make them mushy.

COUSCOUS

2 teaspoons olive oil

1 small onion, diced

1 carrot, diced

$1/2$ acorn squash, peeled, seeded, and diced

2 cups hot Low-Sodium Chicken Stock (page 225)

8 ounces uncooked couscous

3 tablespoons chopped fresh mint

SCALLOPS

2 teaspoons olive oil

20 ounces sea scallops

3 ounces dry white wine

Juice of 1 freshly squeezed lemon

$1^1/2$ cups Low-Sodium Chicken Stock (page 225)

2 tablespoons chopped fresh basil

AUTUMN VEGETABLES

2 teaspoons olive oil

1 yellow zucchini or crookneck squash, sliced on the diagonal $1/4$ inch thick

1 green zucchini, sliced on the diagonal $1/4$ inch thick

2 red bell peppers, seeded and cut into strips 3 inches long by 1 inch wide

4 sprigs thyme, for garnish

To prepare the couscous, heat the olive oil in a saucepan. Add the onions and sauté over medium-high heat for 2 minutes, or until tender. Add the carrot and squash, and continue sautéing for 1 minute. Add the stock and bring to a boil. Stir in the couscous and reduce the heat to low. Cook for 2 minutes, stirring occasionally until the stock has been completely absorbed. Gently stir in the mint and keep warm.

To prepare the scallops, heat the olive oil in a large sauté pan. When the pan is hot, add the scallops and sear over high heat for 1 minute on each side. Add the wine and lemon juice, and simmer for 30 seconds. Remove the scallops from the pan with a slotted spoon and set aside. Add the stock to the pan and reduce by three-quarters, or until the sauce has a thick consistency and coats the back of a spoon. Stir in the basil and keep warm.

To prepare the vegetables, heat the olive oil in a large sauté pan. Add the squash and bell peppers and sauté over medium-high heat for 3 to 4 minutes, until tender and golden brown. Keep warm.

Place a 4-inch round cookie cutter or ring mold in the center of a large dinner plate. Spoon one-quarter of the couscous mixture into the ring and press down to form a round patty. Carefully remove the cookie cutter and repeat for the remaining plates. Fan out the squash and bell peppers on the side of each plate, alternating each and slightly overlapping to create a shingle effect. Arrange the scallops on top of the couscous and spoon the reserved sauce over the scallops and vegetables. Garnish with the thyme and serve immediately.

NUTRITIONAL INFORMATION PER SERVING

Total Calories: 485

Total Fat: 8.6 gm.

Saturated Fat: 1.1 gm.

Cholesterol: 47 mg.

Sodium: 249 mg.

Fiber Rating: 12.6 gm.

❧

NOTE: The scallops we eat are actually the muscle that the scallop used to open and close its shell. Scallops are a calorie bargain at 367 calories per pound. They contain phosphorous, iron, potassium, and some vitamin A, and they are very low in saturated fat.

Poached Orange Roughy with Rhubarb and Riesling Sauce

SERVES: 4

*O*range roughy is an attractive, firm-textured fish that has come into vogue over the last 10 years. In fact, it became too popular, and because of overfishing, catches are now restricted. It is native to the waters of Australia and New Zealand, and until recently it was only available to the North American market in frozen, filleted form. Today, it is widely available fresh. Orange roughy has a pleasantly mild flavor that is similar to sole and flounder, which you can substitute in this recipe. Because it is relatively unassertive in taste, it is helpful to serve it with a sauce of character, which is certainly the case in this recipe. The fruity wine balances the astringent rhubarb, which together with the cranberry juice gives the sauce a colorful ruby hue. If you wish, serve with plain brown rice, or a small portion of Ten-Vegetable Brown Rice (page 120).

SAUCE

3 rhubarb stalks, chopped

1 cup Riesling or other sweet white wine

1 cup low-sodium clam juice

2 tablespoons sugar

1 cup cranberry juice

FISH

1 cup dry white wine

1 cup water

$^1/_2$ carrot, sliced

$^1/_2$ onion, chopped

1 tablespoon chopped shallots

1 bay leaf

4 boneless and skinless orange roughy fillets, 5 to 6 ounces each

Preheat the oven to 375°.

To prepare the sauce, combine the rhubarb, wine, clam juice, sugar, and cranberry juice in a saucepan and bring to a boil over medium heat. Reduce the heat to a simmer and cook for 15 to 18 minutes, until the rhubarb is tender. Transfer the mixture to a blender or food processor and blend until smooth. Return to a clean saucepan and keep warm.

To prepare the fish, combine the wine, water, carrots, onions, shallots, and bay leaf in a large sauté pan. Submerge the fish fillets in the mixture and cover with a tight-fitting lid or a piece of wax paper cut to fit inside the pan exactly. Bring the mixture to a boil over high heat, then immediately transfer the pan to the oven. Cook for 4 to 5 minutes, until the fish is tender and cooked through.

Place the fillets in the center of each serving plate and ladle the sauce around the rim of the plate. Serve immediately.

NOTE: Clam juice can be overly salty. A low-sodium brand makes sense, even for those without special concerns about sodium levels. A homemade fish stock is even better (see page 229).

NUTRITIONAL INFORMATION PER SERVING
Total Calories: 356
Total Fat: 11 gm.
Saturated Fat: 0 gm.
Cholesterol: 34 mg.
Sodium: 180 mg.
Fiber Rating: 1 gm.

Apple Cider-Poached Chicken with Black Currant Barley

SERVES: 4

Apple cider is one of the quintessential fall foods. Though refreshing and delicious on its own, it makes a great poaching liquid and marinade, even for meaty fish like tuna. For pork, I reduce the cider on the stovetop to intensify its flavor and then serve the sauce simply, with a dollop of applesauce. I like to buy fresh apple cider from roadside fruit stands, farmers' markets, local farms, or health food stores, and preferably the unfiltered variety, which tastes like the very essence of apple orchards. The ingredients in this poaching broth may remind you of warm spiced cider, which is basically what it is, and it blends well with the flavor of the black currants.

POACHING BROTH AND CHICKEN

1 red apple, preferably Macintosh or Jonathan, peeled, cored, and diced

5 cups fresh apple cider

1 cinnamon stick, coarsely broken

5 whole cloves

2 whole allspice berries

4 boneless and skinless chicken breasts, about 6 ounces each

BARLEY

$1/2$ tablespoon olive oil

1 tablespoon minced garlic

2 tablespoons minced shallots

1 cup uncooked barley

$2^{1}/_{2}$ cups Low-Sodium Chicken Stock (page 225)

$3/_4$ cup dried black currants

1 tablespoon minced fresh basil

$1/_2$ tablespoon minced fresh oregano

2 tablespoons diced red apple, preferably Macintosh or Jonathan, for garnish

To prepare the broth, combine the apple, cider, cinnamon, cloves, and all-spice in a large saucepan and bring to a boil. Reduce the heat and simmer for 8 to 10 minutes. Reduce the heat to just under a simmer (low enough to stop the broth from simmering but still keeping it hot). Add the chicken breasts and poach for about 15 minutes, or until cooked through. Remove the chicken from the broth and cover with aluminum foil to keep warm.

To prepare the barley, heat the olive oil in a saucepan and sauté the garlic and shallots over medium-high heat for 2 minutes, or until the shallots are translucent. Stir in the barley, add the stock, and simmer over medium-low heat for 20 minutes. Add the currants and continue simmering for 10 minutes longer, or until all the liquid has evaporated. Remove from the heat and stir in the basil and oregano.

Spoon a bed of the barley mixture on each serving plate and place a chicken breast on top. Garnish the chicken with the diced apples.

~

NOTE: Barley is one of the world's oldest grain crops. It has been used as currency and as a standardized measure of weight, as well as a food. It is most commonly used in soups and stews, but as this recipe proves, it also makes a fine side dish. Pearled barley has most of its vitamins and minerals removed in the milling process; hulled barley is not extensively milled and is chewier in texture. One cup of uncooked barley contains 651 calories, 4 grams of fat (of which 0.8 gram. is saturated), 66 grams of fiber, and no cholesterol.

NUTRITIONAL INFORMATION PER SERVING

Total Calories: 504

Total Fat: 9 gm.

Saturated Fat: 2 gm.

Cholesterol: 144 mg.

Sodium: 132 mg.

Fiber Rating: 7 gm.

Chicken and Lobster Ballottine with Melted Leeks and Sundried Tomato Broth

SERVES: 4

Ballottine is the French term for stuffed, rolled, and tied meat or fish, and can be used for limitless combinations of ingredients and stuffings. This dish's hearty, robust flavors—and the availability of lobster—make it most suited to the fall season. It's an elegant way of serving "surf-n-turf," and you can wrap the ballottine ahead of time, which makes it an ideal dish for entertaining.

BALLOTTINE

1 lobster tail (about 4 ounces), shelled and the meat cut into 4 slices, or 2 lobster tails (about 2 ounces each), shelled and the meat cut into 2 slices each

2 boneless and skinless chicken breasts, about 6 ounces each

Juice of $^1/_2$ freshly squeezed lemon

$^1/_4$ teaspoon granulated garlic

Freshly cracked black pepper to taste

8 large spinach leaves

MELTED LEEKS

$^1/_4$ tablespoon olive oil

1 tablespoon minced garlic

4 cups diced leeks, white parts and $^1/_2$ inch of the green parts

$^1/_2$ cup Low-Sodium Chicken Stock (page 225)

1 tablespoon minced fresh tarragon

BROTH

$^1/_4$ tablespoon olive oil

1 teaspoon minced garlic

$^1/_2$ tablespoon finely minced shallots

2 tablespoons chopped sundried tomatoes

$^3/_4$ cup Low-Sodium Chicken Stock (page 225)

Freshly ground black pepper to taste

$^1/_4$ cup chopped fresh basil

4 yellow plum tomatoes, peeled, seeded, and each cut into 8 large-matchstick-sized strips, for garnish (optional)

4 sprigs fresh rosemary, for garnish

To prepare the ballottines, place the lobster tail meat on a metal skewer (or wood skewer soaked in water) to prevent it from curling while cooking. Bring a saucepan of water to a boil, and, using a steamer basket, steam the skewered lobster for 5 to 7 minutes (or 3 to 5 minutes if cooking 2-ounce lobster tails). Do not overcook or the lobster will become tough; it is better cooked a little underdone. Remove the lobster from the steamer and place in an ice bath to cool. Drain and pat dry with paper towels. Set aside.

Place the chicken breasts between 2 large pieces of wax paper. Using a mallet, pound out the breasts until flat and completely even. Season the chicken with the lemon juice, garlic, and pepper. Lay 4 spinach leaves on top of each chicken breast. Place a slice of lobster on top of the spinach in the center of each flattened chicken breast and fold one side of the chicken breast over the lobster. Continue rolling up the chicken breast to enclose the lobster until you form a very tight cylinder or ballottine.

Place each ballottine on a large piece of plastic wrap and roll up, twisting the ends, to create an even tighter cylinder. Place each cylinder on a piece of aluminum foil and tightly roll up again. Twist the ends to secure.

Bring a saucepan of water to a boil. Add the ballottines and poach for about 20 minutes. Remove from the water and keep warm on a plate, wrapped.

Meanwhile, to prepare the leeks, heat the olive oil in a nonstick sauté pan. Add the garlic and leeks and sauté over medium heat for 2 to 3 minutes, until the leeks are tender. Stir in the stock and simmer for 8 to 10 minutes, until almost all of the liquid has evaporated. Remove from the heat, stir in the tarragon, and keep warm.

To prepare the broth, heat the olive oil in a saucepan. Add the garlic and shallots and sauté over medium heat for 2 to 3 minutes. Add the tomatoes and stock, and bring to a boil. Reduce the heat to a simmer and cook for 10 to 15 minutes, or until the tomatoes are very soft. Transfer the mixture to a

NUTRITIONAL
INFORMATION PER
SERVING

Total Calories: 224

Total Fat: 6 gm.

Saturated Fat: 1 gm.

Cholesterol: 66 mg.

Sodium: 148 mg.

Fiber Rating: 3 gm.

blender or food processor and purée until smooth. Strain back into the saucepan and stir in the black pepper and basil.

Unwrap the ballottines and cut on the diagonal into $^1/_4$-inch-thick slices. Arrange the leeks on serving plates in a wide "V" shape. Gently ladle the sauce onto each plate and place the sliced chicken on top of the leeks. Stack the strips of tomato garnish at the apex of the "V" of leeks, garnish the tomato stack with a rosemary sprig, and serve immediately.

NOTE: You can substitute shrimp for the lobster. Using shrimp will increase the cholesterol by 16 milligrams per serving. Both are very low in total fat and low in saturated fat.

Braised Lamb Shank
Pot au Feu

SERVES: 4

*L*amb shank has always been a perennial favorite at the Rittenhouse, in one form or another. This recipe is one of our most popular presentations; we often accompany the lamb shank with wild mushroom risotto and saffron barley. I love the rich and robust flavor of lamb, and especially the intense flavors contained in the shank or foreleg. Because the shank contains thick muscle and connective tissue, it is tough unless braised slowly and for a long time. Prepared correctly, the meat falls off the bone and melts in the mouth. Pot au feu is the classic French preparation of meat and vegetables simmered slowly and gently in a broth. Traditionally, the broth is served as a soup before the meat and vegetables are enjoyed as the main meal.

1 tablespoon olive oil

4 lamb shanks, about 6 ounces each, trimmed of all fat

$^1/_2$ cup red wine

5 cups Low-Sodium Chicken Stock (page 225)

1 bay leaf

2 teaspoons roughly chopped fresh rosemary

1 tablespoon chopped garlic

3 carrots, sliced on the diagonal $^1/_4$ inch thick

1 white onion, cut in quarters

$1^1/_2$ cups diced butternut squash

4 ounces button mushrooms

Preheat the oven to 325°.

Heat the olive oil in a large ovenproof sauté pan with a lid. When the pan is hot, sear the lamb shanks on all sides over high heat for 5 to 6 minutes, or until golden brown. Deglaze the pan with the wine. Add the stock, bay leaf, and rosemary, and bring to a boil. Cover and cook in the oven for 1 hour.

Remove the pan from the oven and add the garlic, carrots, onion, squash, and mushrooms. Cover and continue cooking in the oven for 30 minutes, until the lamb is completely tender.

Ladle the vegetables and broth into a large serving bowl. Arrange the lamb shank in the center of the bowl and garnish with the rosemary placed upright from the middle of the bone.

NUTRITIONAL
INFORMATION PER
SERVING

Total Calories: 383

Total Fat: 13 gm.

Saturated Fat: 4 gm.

Cholesterol: 123 mg.

Sodium: 119 mg.

Fiber Rating: 4 gm.

NOTE: Braising is a moist cooking method that calls for the meat to be browned on all sides and the rendered fat poured off before it is covered and simmered gently with liquid and other ingredients. Moist heat breaks down fibers, keeps the meat moist, and tenderizes it. However, braising is potentially a higher-fat cooking method because the fat remaining in the meat stays in the pot. Be sure to trim the meat of all visible fat before cooking, and drain off the rendered fat after searing the meat.

Roasted Lamb Loin with Fresh Sauerkraut

SERVES: 4

The flavors of lamb and fennel are a natural partnership; lambs love to eat wild fennel if it grows in their pastures. Lamb loin can sometimes be hard to find, in which case I suggest you buy a rack of lamb and trim the loin section off the bone, or ask your butcher to do it for you. I use this sauerkraut recipe at home all the time—it's the best way that I know to prepare cabbage. You can substitute white or red cabbage for the green, if you prefer. Sauerkraut is a national dish of Germany, and a local specialty in the Alsace region of eastern France (where it is called choucroute), but the dish has its origins in China, where cabbage fermented in rice wine was enjoyed thousands of years ago.

LAMB

4 lamb loins, about 4 ounces each, trimmed of all fat and silver skin

1 tablespoon fennel seed, finely ground

1 tablespoon olive oil

SAUERKRAUT

5 cups shredded red cabbage

1 cup white wine vinegar

1 tablespoon caraway seed

1 tablespoon fennel seed

1 tablespoon sugar

32 cooked asparagus spears

4 sprigs oregano, for garnish

Preheat the oven to 400°.

Thoroughly dust the lamb with the ground fennel. Heat the olive oil in an ovenproof sauté pan. When the pan is hot, sear the lamb on all sides until brown. Transfer the pan to the oven and roast for 8 to 10 minutes, until medium-rare to medium.

Meanwhile, place the sauerkraut ingredients in a saucepan and bring to a simmer over medium heat. Cook for 8 to 10 minutes, or until the cabbage is tender.

Place the sauerkraut in a mound in the center of each serving plate. Arrange 8 spears of asparagus around the sauerkraut on each plate like spokes, so the heads of the asparagus lie near the edge of the plate. Slice each lamb loin and arrange slices around the sauerkraut, so the lamb leans a little on the sauerkraut and covers the stalks of the asparagus. Garnish with the thyme sprigs and serve immediately.

NOTE: Sauerkraut is usually high on the list of foods to avoid because, typically, it contains 1,560 milligrams of sodium in just 1 cup—not a heart-healthy ratio! This sauerkraut recipe is fine, because it is made without salt and it's still delicious.

NUTRITIONAL INFORMATION PER SERVING
Total Calories: 289
Total Fat: 13 gm.
Saturated Fat: 4 gm.
Cholesterol: 93 mg.
Sodium: 104 mg.
Fiber Rating: 2 gm.

Apricot-Stuffed Loin of Pork

P ork and fruit are a fabulous combination, as evidenced by the tradi-
tional pork with applesauce. Apricots are another perfect pairing, but
you can use other dried fruits, such as prunes, raisins, currants, or cherries.
As an optional touch, substitute a little of the apple juice with Calvados, the
French apple brandy, or Grand Marnier, the orange liqueur. Serve the pork
with a side dish of braised cabbage, steamed brussels sprouts, rice or quinoa, or
a simple salad.

SERVES: 4

STUFFING

1 teaspoon olive oil

1 tablespoon minced garlic

1 tablespoon minced shallots

$^3/_4$ cup (8 ounces) dried apricots,
    preferably unsulfured, coarsely
    chopped

$^1/_2$ cup apple juice

1 cup fine fresh bread crumbs

Freshly cracked black pepper to taste

1 pork loin, about 22 ounces,
    trimmed of all fat

Preheat the oven to 400°.

To prepare the stuffing, heat the olive oil in a nonstick sauté pan. Add
the garlic and shallots and sauté over medium-high heat for about 3 minutes,
until tender. Add the remaining ingredients and stir together over low heat
until well combined. Remove from the heat and let cool.

Using a long paring knife with a $^1/_2$-inch blade, make an incision into the
center of one end of the pork loin. Gently push the knife toward the center
of the loin, and then twist in a circular motion to form a pocket. Repeat this
process on the other end of the pork loin to create a pocket that runs completely through the loin.

Firmly hold the loin at one end and gently fill the pocket with the stuffing, until full. Repeat the process on the other end. Place the stuffed pork loin in a roasting pan and roast in the oven for 50 minutes to 1 hour, or until the center of the pork reaches an internal temperature of 185°. Remove the pan from the oven and let the pork sit for 5 to 10 minutes.

Carve the pork into $^1/_4$-inch slices and fan out the slices on each serving plate so the stuffing is visible. Add the black pepper to taste, and serve with the side dish of your choice.

NOTE: Apricots are a wonderful source of potassium and vitamin A. Apricots and many other dried fruits are often treated with a sulfur compound to prevent the fruit from darkening. Many people are allergic to sulfur, so try to find unsulfured dried apricots—usually available at health food stores. Unsulfured dried fruit is a little darker in color, but the flavor will be the same.

NUTRITIONAL INFORMATION PER SERVING

Total Calories: 389

Total Fat: 8 gm.

Saturated Fat: 2 gm.

Cholesterol: 111 mg.

Sodium: 145 mg.

Fiber Rating: 5 gm.

Pan-Seared New York Strip with Texas Bean Ragout

It seems like almost every true-blooded Texan has their own variation on a recipe for steak and beans—this one is mine. This is a dish of hearty flavors, and you definitely get your calorie's worth; you will want to make this the main meal of the day, perhaps accompanied by a small plain salad. Confusingly, New York strip is also known as Kansas City steak, Delmonico, sirloin club steak, and shell steak depending on which part of the country you're in. You can spice up this dish by adding your favorite hot sauce, and you can experiment by using different types of beans. Be sure to soak and cook the different types of beans separately, as they have different cooking times.

SERVES: 4

RAGOUT

$^1/_2$ cup dried black beans, rinsed and soaked overnight

$^1/_2$ cup dried navy beans, rinsed and soaked overnight

$^1/_2$ cup dried kidney beans, rinsed and soaked overnight

1 tablespoon minced garlic

2 tablespoons chopped red onions

$^3/_4$ cup Low-Sodium Beef Broth (page 226)

1 teaspoon coarsely chopped fresh rosemary

1 teaspoon coarsely chopped fresh thyme

1 teaspoon coarsely chopped fresh oregano

STEAK

4 New York strip steaks, about 4 ounces each, trimmed of all fat

Freshly cracked black pepper to taste

4 sprigs rosemary, for garnish

To prepare the ragout, drain and rinse the beans and place them into separate saucepans. Cover the beans in each pan with about 1 inch of fresh water and bring to a boil over high heat. Reduce the heat to a simmer and cook the beans for about 45 minutes, or until tender. Drain and set aside.

Coat a large sauté pan with nonstick cooking spray, add the garlic and onions, and sauté over medium heat for 2 minutes, or until the onions are translucent. Stir in the cooked beans and the beef broth, and bring to a boil. Reduce the heat to a simmer and cook the ragout for about 15 minutes, until reduced by one-third. Remove the pan from the heat and stir in the rosemary, thyme, and oregano.

To prepare the steak, coat both sides of each strip with the black pepper. Coat a large nonstick sauté pan with nonstick cooking spray and place over high heat. When the pan is hot, sear the steaks for about $2^1/_2$ minutes on each side, or to the desired doneness.

To serve, spoon a mound of the ragout in the center of each plate, place the steaks on top of the ragout, and garnish with the rosemary sprigs.

NOTE: A large part of the world's population relies on dried beans as a dietary staple, and beans are one of the healthiest foods to add to your diet. They are high in fiber, protein, vitamins, and minerals such as calcium, magnesium, phosphorus, potassium, iron, and zinc, and therefore low in fat. In other words, they are something of a "superfood." Most Americans eat only half the 20 to 30 grams of total fiber needed for good health, approximately one-third of which should come from cholesterol-lowering soluble fiber. Half a cup of cooked and drained black beans, for example, contains 114 calories and 3.6 grams of fiber, with just 0.5 grams of fat.

NUTRITIONAL INFORMATION PER SERVING

Total Calories: 356

Total Fat: 13 gm.

Saturated Fat: 4 gm.

Cholesterol: 83 mg.

Sodium: 85 mg.

Fiber Rating: 18 gm.

Butternut Cheesecake with Poached Cranberries and Lime Zest

SERVES: 6

*W*hen it comes to universal popularity, cheesecake is second to none. The 1980s brought us the pumpkin version for fall, but this recipe refines that recent innovation. The butternut squash purée allows for a more subtle pairing of spices and seasonings, compared to the heavier combination of clove, cinnamon, and allspice that invariably flavors pumpkin cheesecake. Real maple syrup makes a world of difference in all your cooking and baking, or for pouring over pancakes and waffles. It may be more expensive than the flavored syrups that occupy the shelves next to the pancake mixes, but it has an unbeatable taste. The darker, hearty grade B syrup, which is less filtered (and less expensive) than the lighter grade A, also contains valuable nutrients.

CHEESECAKE

1 cup butternut squash, peeled and diced into 1-inch cubes

1 pound nonfat yogurt cheese (page 47)

$^1/_4$ cup brown sugar

$^1/_4$ cup granulated sugar

$^1/_3$ cup nonfat sour cream

1 cup egg substitute (such as Eggbeaters)

$^1/_4$ teaspoon almond extract

Pinch of freshly grated nutmeg

POACHED CRANBERRIES

$^1/_4$ cup water

$^1/_4$ cup granulated sugar

$^1/_4$ cup pure maple syrup

1 cup fresh or frozen cranberries

Juice and minced zest of 1 lime

Preheat the oven to 325°.

To prepare the cheesecake, bring a saucepan of water to a boil. Add the squash and poach for 10 to 15 minutes, or until tender. Transfer to a food processor and purée until smooth. Add the yogurt cheese, brown and granulated sugars, sour cream, egg substitute, almond extract, and nutmeg, and pulse until the cheese is smooth. Run the processor at low speed until the mixture is well combined and thoroughly smooth.

Pour the batter into a 6-inch pan coated with nonstick cooking spray. Place the pan in a water bath and bake in the oven for about 45 minutes, or until a knife inserted into the center comes out clean. Remove from the oven and let cool for 1 hour before unmolding.

Meanwhile, to prepare the cranberries, combine the water, sugar, and maple syrup in a small saucepan and bring to a boil. Stir in the cranberries and cook over medium heat until the first cranberry begins to burst, about 5 or 6 minutes. Remove the pan from the heat, stir in the lime juice and zest, and let sit for 1 hour.

Lower the oven temperature to 200°.

Invert the cheesecake on a plate and tap lightly to remove from the pan. Cut the cheesecake into 6 pieces and place on ovenproof serving plates. Place the plates in the oven and heat just until warm, about 2 minutes. Remove from the oven, spoon the poached cranberries around the cheesecake, and serve immediately.

NOTE: If you serve this dessert without the cranberries, each serving will contain 178 calories and 163 milligrams of sodium; the other values remain unchanged.

NUTRITIONAL
INFORMATION PER
SERVING

Total Calories: 253

Total Fat: 2 gm.

Saturated Fat: 0.4 gm.

Cholesterol: 2 mg.

Sodium: 177 mg.

Fiber Rating: 1 gm.

Black Forest Crepes with Cocoa Sorbet

*T*his dessert adapts the classic Black Forest cake, properly known as Schwarzwälder Kirschtorte, that originated—where else?—in Germany's Black Forest region. That rich and heavy dessert contains chocolate cake soaked in kirsch (cherry liqueur), sour cherries, and kirsch-flavored whipped cream. We have tried to mitigate the high caloric impact of the original by dropping the cream altogether and adapting the flavors of the cake into crepe form. It really works! Also, we capitalize on the fall harvest of wonderful cherries that come from both Michigan and the Pacific Northwest. Cherries and chocolate are a classic natural pairing, and the combination of the other flavors in this recipe is sure to impress your guests.

SERVES: 4

COCOA SORBET

2 cups water

$^2/_3$ cup sugar

2 tablespoons cocoa powder

$^1/_4$ cup freshly squeezed orange juice

1 tablespoon kirsch or other cherry liqueur

CHERRIES

$1^1/_2$ cups pitted cherries

$^1/_2$ tablespoon all-purpose flour

$^1/_2$ cup Merlot or other dry red wine

Minced zest of $^1/_2$ orange

CREPES

$^3/_4$ cup all-purpose flour

2 tablespoons cocoa powder

1 tablespoon sugar

1 tablespoon corn oil

$^1/_3$ cup lowfat (1%) milk

2 egg whites

To prepare the sorbet, combine the water, sugar, and cocoa in a saucepan and bring to a boil, stirring often. Remove the pan from the heat and let cool. Stir in the orange juice and cherry liqueur, and pour into the tub of an ice-cream maker. Freeze according to the manufacturer's directions.

To prepare the cherries, combine all the ingredients in a saucepan, cover, and cook over low heat for about 15 minutes, stirring constantly, until the cherries are tender and the sauce has thickened. Remove from the heat and set aside.

To prepare the crepes, sift the flour, cocoa powder, and sugar into a mixing bowl and set aside. In a separate mixing bowl, combine the corn oil and milk. Slowly add the milk mixture to the flour mixture, stirring constantly to prevent lumping. Whisk the egg whites in a bowl until foamy and fold into the crepe batter.

Heat a nonstick sauté pan until very hot. Pour enough batter to just cover the bottom of the hot pan and let brown for 20 to 30 seconds on each side. Remove the crepe, place on a warm plate, and keep warm. Repeat for the remaining batter. Stack the crepes using pieces of waxed paper to separate each crepe.

Place a large scoop of the sorbet in the center of each serving plate. With a spoon, make a small indentation in the middle of each sorbet. Fold up each crepe like a handkerchief, creating a point with the center of the crepe, and press into the indention in the sorbet. Spoon the cherries over the crepes and the plate and serve immediately.

〜

NOTE: If you love the flavor of chocolate, keep in mind that cocoa powder is much healthier than using chocolate because most of the cocoa butter is removed from the chocolate liquor. One tablespoon of unsweetened cocoa powder contains 21 calories, 0.7 grams of fat (0.4 grams of saturated fat), and no cholesterol or sodium. By comparison, 1 tablespoon of sweet chocolate contains 75 calories, 4.9 grams of fat, and 9 milligrams of sodium.

NUTRITIONAL INFORMATION PER SERVING

Total Calories: 346

Total Fat: 5 gm.

Saturated Fat: 1 gm.

Cholesterol: 1 mg.

Sodium: 45 mg.

Fiber Rating: 1 gm.

Gratin of Apple and Mapled Citrus

Many people raise an eyebrow when they read the word "gratin" on the dessert menu because they think it involves melted cheese. Many gratin dishes do contain cheese, but the term has nothing to do with any particular ingredients; instead, it is used to describe the crust that forms on top of a dish that is baked or broiled. You can freeze the gratin; the gelatin ensures that it will not separate or leech water when defrosted. Instead of preparing it in individual serving bowls, freeze the gratin in a shallow baking pan. Simply thaw the dish in the refrigerator before dividing into servings.

SERVES: 4

$^1/_2$ teaspoon plus 1 tablespoon maple extract

1 tablespoon Karo syrup

1 grapefruit, peeled and sectioned

1 large green apple, peeled, cored, and cut into large dice

$^1/_2$ tablespoon unflavored gelatin

$^1/_4$ cup cold water

1 cup nonfat yogurt cheese (page 47) or nonfat ricotta cheese

$^1/_2$ cup sugar

Minced zest of $^1/_2$ orange

3 egg whites

8 sections grapefruit, membranes removed, for garnish

4 mint sprigs, for garnish

Preheat the oven to 350°.

To prepare the gratin, combine $^1/_2$ teaspoon of the maple extract, the Karo syrup, grapefruit, and apple in a mixing bowl and marinate for 1 hour. Transfer the marinated fruit into 4 shallow, heat-resistant serving bowls and set aside.

Place the cold water in the top of a double boiler. Sprinkle the gelatin over the water and heat over simmering water, stirring constantly until the gelatin is dissolved.

Using a rubber spatula, thoroughly mix together the cheese, $^1/_4$ cup of the sugar, the orange zest, and the remaining 1 tablespoon of maple extract in a mixing bowl. In a separate mixing bowl, whisk together the egg whites and the remaining $^1/_4$ cup of sugar until stiff peaks form. Fold into the cheese mixture, and then stir in the dissolved gelatin. Pour the mixture over the marinated fruit in the serving bowls, making sure to fully cover the fruit. Smooth out the top with the back of a spoon and refrigerate until chilled.

Prepare the broiler. Place the serving bowls on the top rack of the broiler and broil for 1 to 2 minutes under high heat, until the top of the desserts are lightly browned. Garnish each gratin with 2 grapefruit sections and a mint sprig, and serve immediately.

NUTRITIONAL INFORMATION PER SERVING

Total Calories: 196

Total Fat: 0.3 gm.

Saturated Fat: 0.1 gm.

Cholesterol: 1 mg.

Sodium: 107 mg.

Fiber Rating: 2 gm.

NOTE: Maple extract is available in bottles, like vanilla extract. Karo syrup, made from corn, contains 60 calories per tablespoon, 30 milligrams of sodium, and no fat or cholesterol.

Poached Asian Pears with Lemon-Ginger-and Anise-Flavored Fruit Compote

SERVES: 4

This dessert has proved very popular on the fall menu at the Rittenhouse. Asian pears (also known as Chinese pears) apple pears, sand pears, and Nashi (the Japanese word for pear), are round in shape, wonderfully crisp and crunchy, and refreshingly juicy. There are many different varieties, so they may vary in size and color from one batch to the next. Asian pears are a fairly recent addition to the fruit section of our stores—I saw them for the first time on a trip to China in the 1980s—but fortunately, their popularity has made them easily available across the United States. They are less acidic than regular pears and keep their texture well when poached. The compote is flavored with Asian ingredients such as ginger and star anise that perfectly complement the pears.

1/4 cup sugar

2 cups water

1/2 cup minced fresh ginger

1 lemon, cut in half

2 star anise

1 cup sweet dessert wine

4 Asian pears, peeled and cored

1/2 cup blueberries

1/2 cup sliced strawberries

1/2 cup diced plums

1/2 cup diced peaches

4 mint sprigs

Place the sugar, water, ginger, lemon halves, star anise, and wine in a large saucepan and bring to a boil. Add the pears and reduce the heat to medium-low. Simmer, uncovered, for 30 to 45 minutes, stirring occasionally, until the pears are tender. Remove the pears and set aside.

Strain the poaching liquid into a clean pan and bring to a boil. When the liquid thickens and becomes syrupy, add the blueberries, strawberries, plums, and peaches, and coat well.

Place the fruit compote in the center of each serving plate and place the pears in the middle of the compote. Garnish each pear with a mint sprig, and serve.

NOTE: Asian pears are a good source of vitamin C. They are hard to the touch even when ripe, and they store very well in the refrigerator for a week or two.

NUTRITIONAL INFORMATION PER SERVING

Total Calories: 278

Total Fat: 1 gm.

Saturated Fat: 0 gm.

Cholesterol: 0 mg.

Sodium: 8 mg.

Fiber Rating: 6.2 gm.

Winter

⌒ APPETIZERS ⌒

Winter Harvest Vegetable Soup with Chive Yogurt / 152

Wild Mushroom and Salsify in Phyllo with Tarragon Jus / 154

Polenta with Roasted Pepper and Artichoke Ragout / 157

Chicken and Roasted Walnut Risotto with Spinach Coulis / 159

⌒ SALADS ⌒

Warm Duo of Cabbage Salad with Mustard Vinaigrette / 161

Endive and Red Oak Salad with Walnut Vinaigrette / 163

Tossed Hearts of Romaine with a Trio of Peppers and Honey-Lemon Dressing / 164

⌒ ENTRÉES ⌒

Kidney Bean, Root Vegetable, and Barley Chili-Stuffed Baked Acorn Squash / 165

Oat Bran and Dill–Crusted Red Snapper with Cinnamon Spaghetti Squash / 168

Herb-Rubbed Whole Roasted Capon with Sweet Potato Purée / 170

Salmon en Papillote with Julienne of Vegetables and Fresh Shallots / 173

Pan-Roasted Pheasant Breast with Braised Apples and Cabbage / 175

Beef Medallions with Port and Sweet Onion Sauce and Potato-Leek Pierogis / 178

⌒ DESSERTS ⌒

Pear and Pistachio Strudel with Oregano-Almond Crust / 181

Banana-Anise Tofulato Sundae with Black Walnut Praline and Cocoa Glaze / 184

Upside-Down Caribbean Mango Gingerbread / 186

Baked Apples Stuffed with Indian Pudding and Stewed Apricots / 188

Opposite: Oat Bran and Dill–Crusted Red Snapper with Cinnamon Spaghetti Squash, page 168.

Winter Harvest Vegetable Soup with Chive Yogurt

SERVES: 4

*W*inter is the season to enjoy hearty, nourishing soups, and I enjoy making them regularly at home for my family, as well as for my hotel guests. We invariably feature a seasonal vegetable soup at the Rittenhouse. In days gone by, this may have been more challenging during winter. These days, with California and foreign produce easily available, there is an attractive array of vegetables whatever the time of year. If you want to turn this soup into a more substantial dish—as a filling lunch, for example—add some cooked beans and serve with a rustic five-grain or whole-wheat bread.

SOUP

1 tablespoon olive oil

1 tablespoon minced garlic

$^1/_3$ cup diced onions

$^1/_3$ cup diced carrots

$^1/_3$ cup diced leeks (white part only)

$^1/_3$ cup diced yellow squash

$^1/_3$ cup diced zucchini

$^1/_3$ cup seeded and diced red bell pepper

$^1/_3$ cup seeded and diced green bell pepper

1 potato (about 6 ounces), peeled and diced

$^1/_3$ cup broccoli florets

6 cups Low-Sodium Chicken Stock (page 225)

1 bay leaf

$^1/_3$ cup diced tomato

1 tablespoon minced fresh rosemary

1 tablespoon minced fresh parsley

1 tablespoon freshly cracked black pepper

CHIVE YOGURT

$^1/_4$ cup nonfat plain yogurt

1 tablespoon sliced fresh chives

To prepare the soup, heat the olive oil in a saucepan and add the garlic, onions, carrots, and leeks. Sauté over medium heat for about 2 minutes, until the onion is translucent. Add the yellow squash, zucchini, bell peppers, potato, broccoli, and stock, and bring to a boil. Add the bay leaf, reduce the heat to medium-low, and simmer for 20 minutes. Remove the bay leaf and discard. Stir in the tomatoes, rosemary, parsley, and pepper.

Transfer the mixture to a blender or food processor and purée until smooth. Return the soup to a clean saucepan and bring to a low boil before serving.

Thoroughly mix together the yogurt and chives in a mixing bowl. Ladle the soup into serving bowls and garnish each serving with a dollop of the chive yogurt.

NUTRITIONAL INFORMATION PER SERVING
Total Calories: 104
Total Fat: 4 gm.
Saturated Fat: 0.5 gm.
Cholesterol: 0.3 mg.
Sodium: 54 mg.
Fiber Rating: 2 gm.

NOTE: The savory yogurt gives the soup some richness and makes a good, heart-healthy substitute for the more usual sour cream or crème fraîche. Many people who are lactose-intolerant are able to eat yogurt because the acid-producing bacteria it contains breaks down the sugar in milk (lactose) into a simple form. If you wish, you can thicken yogurt by straining out the excess fluid with a coffee filter or cheesecloth (see page 47).

Wild Mushroom and Salsify in Phyllo with Tarragon Jus

SERVES: 6

Salsify is a parsnip-shaped cream-colored winter root vegetable that is popular in Europe, especially in Mediterranean countries such as Italy, Spain, and Greece. Salsify is also known as vegetable oyster because of its delicate flavor, although it doesn't taste like oysters to me—it's more reminiscent of artichokes. To prepare salsify, just wash and peel it; the leaves are also edible and can be added to salads or steamed. Salsify works well as a partner for mushrooms; using a selection of different mushrooms diversifies their flavors. However, if only one or two types are available, increase the amounts accordingly. Their dense and meaty richness is balanced and cut by the herbal sharpness of the tarragon jus.

FILLING

1/2 cup peeled and diced salsify

1 tablespoon minced garlic

1 tablespoon minced shallots

1 cup sliced button mushrooms

1 cup shiitake mushrooms stemmed and sliced

1 cup portobello mushrooms stemmed and sliced

1 cup sliced cremini mushrooms, or additional shiitakes

1/4 cup dry white wine

1/4 cup Low-Sodium Chicken Stock (page 225)

1/4 cup sliced scallions

1 tablespoon chopped fresh tarragon

1 tablespoon minced fresh parsley

1 tablespoon minced fresh rosemary

PHYLLO

4 sheets phyllo dough

TARRAGON JUS

2 cups Low-Sodium Beef Broth (page 226)

1 teaspoon minced garlic

1 teaspoon minced shallots

1/4 cup chopped fresh tarragon

1 tablespoon cornstarch

1 tablespoon dry white wine

To prepare the filling, coat a sauté pan with nonstick cooking spray. Add the salsify and sauté over medium-high heat for about 2 minutes. Add the garlic and shallots, and continue sautéing for 1 minute. Stir in the mushrooms and sauté for 2 to 3 minutes, until all the liquid has evaporated. Deglaze the pan with the wine. Add the stock, scallions, tarragon, parsley, and rosemary, and continue cooking over high heat until almost all of the liquid has evaporated, about 5 minutes. Remove the pan from the heat and let cool.

Preheat the oven to 400°.

Lay out a sheet of the phyllo dough on a flat work surface and lightly brush with water. Top with another phyllo sheet, brush with water, and repeat with the remaining phyllo sheets, stacking them as you go. Cut the stacked phyllo into 6 equal squares, and spoon about $1/4$ cup of the filling in the center of each square. Bring the corners of each square inwards, meeting in the center, and then pinch the dough to seal it tightly. Transfer the phyllo to a baking sheet coated with nonstick cooking spray and bake in the oven for 10 to 15 minutes, until golden brown.

To prepare the jus, combine the beef broth, garlic, and shallots in a small saucepan and bring to a boil. Reduce the heat to a simmer and stir in the tarragon. Mix together the cornstarch and wine in a cup, and then whisk into the jus. Continue simmering for 5 minutes, whisking occasionally, until the jus thickens.

To serve, ladle about $1/2$ cup of the jus in the center of each serving bowl. Place the phyllo on top of the jus and serve immediately.

❧

NOTES: Salsify is a poor source of vitamins, but $1/2$ cup of the cooked vegetable contains 32 milligrams of calcium and 192 milligrams of potassium. It has negligible fat, no saturated fat, and no cholesterol.

NUTRITIONAL INFORMATION PER SERVING

Total Calories: 85

Total Fat: 3 gm.

Saturated Fat: 0.4 gm.

Cholesterol: 53 mg.

Sodium: 13 mg.

Fiber Rating: 1 gm.

Polenta with Roasted Pepper and Artichoke Ragout

SERVES: 4

This is a rustic appetizer that's best enjoyed in front of a roaring fire on a cold winter evening. Artichokes are the unopened flower buds of a plant in the thistle family. Polenta is a hearty, filling dish that's a staple in northern Italy. It warms the body and sticks to the ribs, somewhat like oatmeal porridge. The eye-catching presentation with colorful greens, yellows, and reds will make you think of the sunny cuisine of the Mediterranean—the perfect antidote for winter. Do not use canned artichoke hearts, which contain high levels of sodium.

POLENTA

$1^{1}/_{2}$ cups coarse yellow cornmeal

$1^{1}/_{2}$ cups nonfat milk

$1^{1}/_{2}$ cups Low-Sodium Chicken Stock (page 225)

$^{1}/_{4}$ cup dry white wine

$1^{1}/_{2}$ tablespoons minced garlic

$1^{1}/_{2}$ tablespoons minced shallots

$1^{1}/_{2}$ tablespoons chopped fresh dill

$1^{1}/_{2}$ tablespoons chopped fresh parsley

RAGOUT

1 teaspoon olive oil

1 tablespoon minced garlic

1 tablespoon minced shallots

2 red bell peppers, roasted, peeled, seeded, and sliced into strips

2 green bell peppers, roasted, peeled, seeded, and sliced into strips

$1^{1}/_{4}$ cups diced fresh or frozen artichoke hearts

$^{1}/_{4}$ cup coarsely chopped fresh basil

1 tablespoon chopped fresh dill

2 tablespoons dry white wine

Freshly cracked black pepper to taste

4 dill sprigs, for garnish

To prepare the polenta, mix together the cornmeal and milk in a mixing bowl and set aside. Combine the remaining polenta ingredients in a nonstick saucepan and bring to a boil. Slowly whisk in the cornmeal mixture. Reduce the heat to medium-low and, stirring constantly with a wooden spoon, cook the mixture for 12 to 15 minutes, until the mixture thickens and starts to pull away from the pan.

Line a 9-inch square baking pan with plastic wrap. Pour the polenta into the pan, spread out evenly, and set aside to cool. Cut the cooled polenta into 12 squares of different sizes, as follows: four 3-inch squares; four 2-inch squares; and four 1-inch squares. Set aside.

Preheat the oven to 400°.

To prepare the ragout, heat the olive oil in a nonstick sauté pan. Add the garlic and shallots, and sauté over medium heat for about 2 minutes, being careful not to burn the mixture. Add the roasted bell peppers and artichokes, and sauté for 2 minutes longer. Add the basil, dill, white wine, and pepper, and continue cooking for about 5 minutes, until most of the liquid has evaporated. Keep warm.

Meanwhile, place the polenta squares on a baking sheet coated with nonstick cooking spray and place in the oven for 2 to 3 minutes, until heated through.

To serve, place the largest (3-inch) polenta squares on the left-hand side of each serving plate and spoon some of the ragout on top. Add the medium-sized (2-inch) polenta squares on top and spoon with more of the ragout. Top with the smallest (1-inch squares) and more ragout. Spoon the remaining ragout on the right-hand side of each plate and serve immediately.

NUTRITIONAL
INFORMATION PER
SERVING

Total Calories: 278

Total Fat: 3 gm.

Saturated Fat: 0.5 gm.

Cholesterol: 2 gm.

Sodium: 120 mg.

Fiber Rating: 8 gm.

Chicken and Roasted Walnut Risotto with Spinach Coulis

*L*ike the polenta in the previous recipe, risotto is a filling and warming winter dish. The trick to a perfect risotto is to add the stock in increments, stirring all the while, and to wait for it to be absorbed before adding more. The rice will take on a creamy consistency, yet the grains will remain firm and distinctly separate. It's also important to use the Italian short-grain Arborio rice because its high starch content contributes to the dish's creamy texture. Toasted nuts of all kinds make good additions to risottos, because their crunchy texture contrasts with the other, softer ingredients. In this recipe, the toasted walnuts, chicken, and rosemary provide a rustic and flavorful combination, while the coulis makes a striking visual contrast with the rest of the dish.

SERVES: 4

SPINACH COULIS

3 cups tightly packed fresh spinach

$^1/_4$ cup Low-Sodium Chicken Stock (page 225)

1 teaspoon minced garlic

1 teaspoon minced shallots

$^1/_2$ cup fresh basil leaves

Pinch of freshly cracked black pepper

RISOTTO

2 boneless and skinless chicken breasts, about 5 ounces each, finely diced

1 tablespoon minced garlic

1 tablespoon minced shallots

2 cups uncooked Arborio rice

5 cups Low-Sodium Chicken Stock (page 225)

2 tablespoons chopped fresh rosemary

2 bay leaves

1 tablespoon walnuts, toasted and coarsely chopped

$^1/_3$ cup chopped fresh parsley

$^1/_4$ teaspoon salt

Pinch of freshly cracked black pepper

NUTRITIONAL
INFORMATION PER
SERVING

Total Calories: 444

Total Fat: 4 gm.

Saturated Fat: 1 gm.

Cholesterol: 32 mg.

Sodium: 203 mg.

Fiber Rating: 2 gm.

To prepare the coulis, bring a saucepan of water to a boil. Add the spinach and quickly blanch for 30 seconds. Remove the spinach with a slotted spoon and drain thoroughly. Transfer to a blender or food processor, add the remaining coulis ingredients, and purée until very smooth. Keep warm.

To prepare the risotto, coat a sauté pan with nonstick cooking spray. When the pan is hot, add the diced chicken and, stirring occasionally, sauté over medium heat for 2 to 3 minutes, until golden brown. Add the garlic and shallots, and continue to sauté for 30 seconds. With a wooden spoon, stir in the rice and cook for 15 seconds. Stir in $1^2/_3$ cups of the stock and the rosemary and bay leaves and continue stirring with the wooden spoon until all the liquid has been absorbed. Add another $1^2/_3$ cups of the stock and stir constantly until the liquid has been absorbed again. Add the remaining $1^2/_3$ cups of the stock, stir in the walnuts and parsley, and continue to stir until all the liquid has been absorbed and the risotto is thick and creamy. If the rice is still crunchy, add a little more stock and continue cooking. Season with the salt and pepper.

To serve, spoon a mound of the risotto in the center of each serving plate and drizzle with the coulis.

NOTE: Spinach originated in Persia. North African Moors loved it so much they called it the prince of vegetables. Although spinach is high in calcium, the body cannot use most of it because it is chelated, or bound with another compound (oxalic acid) that blocks its absorption.

Warm Duo of Cabbage Salad with Mustard Vinaigrette

SERVES: 4

For this recipe you will need to cook the two types of cabbage in separate pans (or cook one type of cabbage at a time) to avoid the red cabbage bleeding into the white. If you have an artistic eye, you may want to present the salad in a yin-yang shape by placing aluminum foil in an "S" shape inside a large, round cutter, filling each side with a different cabbage, and then gently removing the mold. This salad reminds me of a dish I demonstrated years ago when I traveled on an exchange with foreign chefs—a smoked shrimp chile relleno with a warm cabbage salad and crayfish. It was notably calorific and not at all heart-healthy, laden with bacon, blue cheese, and cream. This is my contemporary, cleaned-up version. Serve it with leftover turkey or fish to make a filling lunch.

MUSTARD VINAIGRETTE

1 teaspoon rice wine vinegar

1 tablespoon Dijon mustard

1 teaspoon minced garlic

1 teaspoon minced shallot

1 tablespoon olive oil

1 tablespoon Low-Sodium Chicken Stock (page 225)

$^{1}/_{2}$ tablespoon chopped fresh parsley

SALAD

3 tablespoons minced garlic

3 tablespoons minced shallots

3 cups red cabbage cut into 1-inch dice

3 cups white cabbage cut into 1-inch dice

4 tablespoons unseasoned rice wine vinegar

4 tablespoons Low-Sodium Chicken Stock (page 225)

1 teaspoon sugar

To prepare the vinaigrette, whisk together the vinegar, mustard, garlic, and shallot in a mixing bowl. Slowly whisk in the oil, then whisk in the stock and parsley, until emulsified. Set aside.

To prepare the salad, coat 2 sauté pans with nonstick cooking spray. Add half of the garlic and shallots to each pan and sauté over medium heat for 1 minute. Add the red cabbage to one pan and the white cabbage to the other. Add half of the vinegar, stock, and sugar to each pan and sauté over medium-high heat for 4 or 5 minutes, until all the liquid has evaporated.

Arrange each cabbage in adjoining mounds on serving plates or form into an attractive pattern. Drizzle with the vinaigrette.

NOTE: For many people the main event of the salad course is a high-calorie, taste-smothering, fatty dressing. This vinaigrette has only about 60 calories. Use it to marinate turkey steaks for grilling, as a simple dipping sauce for sliced cucumbers, or to dress blanched and chilled green beans.

NUTRITIONAL
INFORMATION PER
SERVING

Total Calories: 75

Total Fat: 4 gm.

Saturated Fat: 0.5 gm.

Cholesterol: 0

Sodium: 72 mg.

Fiber Rating: 2 gm.

Endive and Red Oak Salad with Walnut Vinaigrette

*T*his is a simple, clean-flavored, refreshing winter salad that is ideally paired with a meat entrée. The two main salad greens make a good contrast with the slightly bitter, smooth endive and the leafy, crisp red oak lettuce. The aromatic walnut oil gives the salad a hearty, nutty flavor. It is important that the vinegar used with the oil be mild and unassertive so the two ingredients don't compete. Walnut oil has a wonderful, unique flavor—buy a small bottle and make it an occasional treat.

SERVES: 4

WALNUT VINAIGRETTE

¹/₂ tablespoon Champagne vinegar or unseasoned rice wine vinegar

¹/₂ teaspoon minced garlic

¹/₂ teaspoon minced shallot

Pinch of freshly cracked black pepper

¹/₂ tablespoon walnut oil

¹/₂ tablespoon olive oil

3 tablespoons Low-Sodium Chicken Stock (page 225)

1 tablespoon chopped walnuts

1 tablespoon chopped fresh parsley

SALAD

1 ounce Belgian endive (about 5 or 6 spears)

2 ounces baby red oak lettuce (about 2 cups), or chopped red oak lettuce

NUTRITIONAL INFORMATION PER SERVING

Total Calories: 46

Total Fat: 5 gm.

Saturated Fat: 0.5 gm.

Cholesterol: 0

Sodium: 2 mg.

Fiber Rating: 0.4 gm.

To prepare the vinaigrette, whisk together the vinegar, garlic, shallots, and black pepper in a mixing bowl and let steep for 5 to 10 minutes. Slowly whisk in the walnut and olive oils until emulsified. Then, slowly whisk in the stock until emulsified, and whisk in the walnuts and parsley. Slice each endive spear into 4 strips lengthwise and arrange on each serving plate in a star shape. Mound the lettuce in the center of each plate and drizzle with the vinaigrette.

Tossed Hearts of Romaine with a Trio of Peppers and Honey-Lemon Dressing

SERVES: 4

This straightforward, colorful salad makes a great appetizer on its own, or you can serve it with fowl, which makes it ideal to have on hand during the holiday season. You can substitute Bibb, frisée, or another sturdy lettuce for the romaine, but avoid delicate greens such as baby spinach, mâche, or a mesclun mix. You will only need the tender romaine hearts for this recipe, but you can store and use the outer leaves for other salads. The lemon and honey make a classic sweet and sour dressing, and you can use it with all types of salads.

NUTRITIONAL
INFORMATION PER
SERVING

Total Calories: 45

Total Fat: 0.1 gm.

Saturated Fat: 0 gm.

Cholesterol: 0 mg.

Sodium: 2 mg.

Fiber Rating: 1 gm.

HONEY-LEMON DRESSING

Juice of 2 freshly squeezed lemons

1 tablespoon honey (or to taste)

$^1/_2$ tablespoon chopped fresh
   rosemary

SALAD

$^1/_2$ small red bell pepper, roasted,
   peeled, seeded, and julienned

$^1/_2$ small yellow bell pepper, roasted,
   peeled, seeded, and julienned

$^1/_2$ small green bell pepper, roasted,
   peeled, seeded, and julienned

$2^1/_2$ ounces romaine hearts (from
   about 2 heads)

Thoroughly whisk together all the dressing ingredients in a small mixing bowl. To prepare the salad, place the julienned bell peppers and romaine hearts in a mixing bowl. Toss with the dressing. To serve, layer the romaine and bell pepper strips in a mound in the center of each serving plate.

NOTE: This recipe uses honey not only for sweetness and to balance the acidity of the lemon, but also to help the dressing cling to the salad.

Kidney Bean, Root Vegetable, and Barley Chili-Stuffed Baked Acorn Squash

*T*his recipe is a variation on a popular winter vegetarian menu item at the Rittenhouse, and trust me, it's a full meal! Serving the chile inside the oval, orange-fleshed acorn squash makes a great presentation and a sure-fire conversation piece for any dinner party. You can vary the mix of root vegetables, and you can spice up the chili by adding jalapeños or hot sauce. This recipe is particularly convenient for entertaining because you can make the chili ahead of time and then stuff and bake the squash at the last minute.

$^1/_2$ cup dried kidney or pinto beans, rinsed and soaked overnight

7 cups water

4 cups uncooked barley

6 small acorn squash (about 18 to 20 ounces each)

1 teaspoon olive oil

$^1/_2$ cup diced onions

$^1/_2$ cup diced carrots

$^1/_3$ cup diced daikon, celeriac, or salsify

$^1/_3$ cup diced taro, rutabaga, or parsnip

$^1/_3$ cup diced butternut squash

2 tablespoons ground cumin

2 tablespoons pure red chile powder

2 cups canned tomatoes, drained and diced

$1^1/_2$ cups Low-Sodium Chicken Stock (page 225)

$^1/_2$ cup sliced scallions

$^1/_2$ teaspoon freshly cracked black pepper

2 tablespoons chopped fresh cilantro

12 scallions, for garnish (optional)

Drain and rinse the beans and place in a saucepan. Add 4 cups of the water (or enough to cover the beans by 1 inch) and bring to a boil over high heat. Reduce the heat to a simmer and cook for 40 minutes, or until tender. Drain the beans and transfer to a mixing bowl.

Meanwhile, place the barley in a saucepan with the remaining 3 cups of water and bring to a boil over high heat. Reduce the heat to a simmer and cook for 12 to 15 minutes, until tender. Drain the barley and transfer to the bowl with the beans. Toss the cooked beans and barley together and set aside.

Preheat the oven to 400°.

Cut the squash in half lengthwise. Place the squash, cut-side up, in an ovenproof baking dish and add enough water to come $^1/_4$ inch up the sides of the squash. Cover with aluminum foil and par-bake in the oven for 15 minutes. Remove from the oven and scoop out all the seeds and a little of the flesh, leaving about a 1-inch thickness of flesh in the squash. Set aside. Lower the oven temperature to 375°.

Heat the olive oil in a saucepan. Add the onions, carrots, daikon, taro, and butternut squash and sweat over medium heat for 2 minutes. Stir in the cumin, chile powder, and tomatoes and cook for 2 minutes longer. Add the stock, scallions, and pepper and simmer for 20 minutes, or until almost all the liquid has evaporated. Remove the pan from the heat and gently stir in the cilantro.

Thoroughly stir the vegetable mixture into the bean and barley mixture. Spoon the filling into the par-baked acorn squash and bake in the oven for about 15 minutes, or until the squash is tender. Remove from the oven and place each squash on a serving plate. Angle the squash a little so the filling flows out onto the plate. Place the scallions upright on one side of the squash to garnish, and serve immediately.

NOTE: Don't let the elevated calorie count alarm you—this dish is meant to be an entire meal. A typical main meal with meat, starch, and a vegetable would most likely be higher in calories. This recipe is a terrific source of fiber, thanks to the beans and barley. One cup of dry barley contains 31 grams of fiber, and 1 cup of cooked beans contains 14 grams.

NUTRITIONAL
INFORMATION PER
SERVING

Total Calories: 509

Total Fat: 4 gm.

Saturated Fat: 1 gm.

Cholesterol: 0 mg.

Sodium: 159 mg.

Fiber Rating: 24 gm.

Oat Bran and Dill–Crusted Red Snapper with Cinnamon Spaghetti Squash

SERVES: 4

*H*ere is another popular heart-healthy item from the Rittenhouse winter menu. The oats and dill make a robust crust that can also be used to sauté other firm-fleshed fish such as flounder or striped bass. Spaghetti squash is remarkable in that the cooked flesh not only separates into pasta-like strands but can be used in the same way, with sauces and toppings. It has little flavor of its own, so it needs to be accompanied by assertive ingredients, whether savory, such as herbs and spices, or sweet, as in this case.

SQUASH

1 spaghetti squash (about 1 pound)

$^1/_2$ tablespoon ground cinnamon

1 tablespoon honey

1 tablespoon minced fresh dill

CRUST

1 cup oat bran

$^3/_4$ cup minced fresh dill

$^3/_4$ tablespoons powdered garlic

$^1/_4$ teaspoon freshly ground white pepper

4 skinless red snapper fillets, about 6 ounces each

Preheat the oven to 400°.

To prepare the squash, slice off each end and cut the squash in half lengthwise. Remove the seeds with a large spoon and place both pieces of squash in a large casserole dish, cut side down. Fill the dish half-full with water and bake the squash in the oven for about 1 hour, or until the flesh is soft.

Remove the squash from the dish and let cool slightly. Spoon out the flesh and place in a mixing bowl. Add the cinnamon, honey, and dill, and toss together until combined. Keep warm.

Lower the oven temperature to 375°.

Mix together all the crust ingredients in a mixing bowl. Liberally coat both sides of the snapper fillets with the crust mixture. Heat a nonstick sauté pan coated with nonstick cooking spray and, when the pan is hot, add the snapper. Sauté over medium-high heat for 3 to 4 minutes on each side, until golden brown. Transfer the fillets to a nonstick baking sheet coated with nonstick cooking spray and finish cooking in the oven for 8 to 10 minutes.

Transfer the snapper to serving plates and serve with the squash.

NOTE: Reducing your intake of saturated fat and cholesterol along with increasing your intake of fiber (with emphasis on getting at least 10 grams of soluble fiber per day) are all wise approaches to reducing your risk of heart disease. Oat bran is one of the many excellent sources of soluble fiber.

NUTRITIONAL INFORMATION PER SERVING

Total Calories: 295

Total Fat: 5 gm.

Saturated Fat: 1 gm.

Cholesterol: 63 mg.

Sodium: 115 mg.

Fiber Rating: 6 gm.

Herb-Rubbed Whole Roasted Capon with Sweet Potato Purée

SERVES: 4

Capons are young roosters that have been neutered when immature and fattened to improve their flavor. They usually weigh between 6 and 10 pounds and yield juicy, tender meat. They make a welcome change from chicken and the common holiday turkey, yet they are large enough to provide leftovers for sandwiches, soups, and stews. At the Rittenhouse we are fortunate to have a local supply of free-range capons that come from the cleanest poultry farm you'll ever see, in Lancaster County, Pennsylvania. As with chicken and turkey, free-range birds are well worth the investment in terms of flavor, texture, and healthfulness. The lemon stuffing was perfected by Greg Slonaker, one of our line cooks, who tested many of these recipes; it's based on a technique I read about in some old Italian cookbooks. The lemon stuffing and herb crust make a wonderfully aromatic and intense flavor combination.

CAPON

2 lemons

1 capon (about 6 pounds)

2 tablespoons finely minced garlic

$1/2$ tablespoon freshly cracked black pepper

$1/3$ cup chopped mixed fresh herbs, such as thyme, rosemary, sage, and parsley

SWEET POTATO PURÉE

6 cups diced sweet potatoes

$1/4$ cup honey

2 teaspoons cayenne pepper powder

1 teaspoon ground nutmeg

Freshly cracked black pepper to taste

Preheat the oven to 375°.

To prepare the capon, roll the lemons on a work surface while exerting downward pressure to release the pulp and juice inside the fruit. Puncture the lemons with a fork and place inside the capon's cavity. Rub the capon generously with the garlic and black pepper and sprinkle the herbs over the outside, gently patting so they adhere.

Transfer the capon to a roasting pan and roast in the oven for $1^{1}/_{2}$ to $1^{3}/_{4}$ hours, or until the juices run clear. Remove from the oven and let rest for 10 to 15 minutes before carving.

Meanwhile, to prepare the sweet potatoes, bring a large saucepan of salted water to a boil. Add the sweet potatoes and boil for 15 to 18 minutes, until soft. Drain the potatoes and place in a mixing bowl. Add the remaining ingredients and beat with an electric mixer or mash by hand until smooth.

Carve the capon. Place about $^{1}/_{2}$ cup of the puréed sweet potatoes in a mound in the center of each serving plate and arrange slices of the capon around the potatoes; allow about 4 ounces of capon breast meat per person.

NOTE: Sweet potatoes are an excellent source of vitamins A and C, beta-carotene, and potassium. Each $^{1}/_{2}$ cup serving of the sweet potato purée contains 172 calories.

NUTRITIONAL
INFORMATION PER
SERVING

Total Calories: 546

Total Fat: 10 gm.

Saturated Fat: 3 gm.

Cholesterol: 96 mg.

Sodium: 113 mg.

Fiber Rating: 7 gm.

Salmon en Papillote with Julienne of Vegetables and Fresh Shallots

SERVES: 4

ooking "en papillote" is a classic French technique for baking food, usually fish, inside a sealed wrapping of parchment paper. Originally, this cooking method was mainly used for veal, and the paper package was cut into a heart shape, which seems like a nice touch. The moisture inside the package forms steam when heated in the oven, which puffs up the package until it is cut open at the table. En papillote is a marvelous way to cook delicate fish such as sole, snapper, and flounder, because the steam prevents them from drying out. The first time I ever ate food that had been cooked by this method was at The Commander's Palace, the eminent New Orleans restaurant. I was 16, and very impressed, and I couldn't wait to try it again.

4 salmon fillets, about 7 ounces each

$^1/_4$ cup julienned carrots

$^1/_4$ cup julienned daikon

$^1/_4$ cup seeded and julienned red bell pepper

$^1/_4$ cup finely chopped shallots

$^1/_2$ cup dry white wine

Freshly cracked black pepper to taste

Preheat the oven to 375°.

Lay out 4 pieces of parchment paper on a work surface. Fold the paper in half and cut off the top two corners in a curved shape to form half-moons. Open the paper and place the salmon in the middle of the right-hand side of the paper, crimping the edge of the paper to hold in the ingredients. Place the remaining ingredients on top of the salmon. Fold over the other side of the parchment paper and crimp the edges together by hand or secure with a paper clip to form a sealed package.

Place the packages on a baking sheet, transfer to the oven, and bake for 10 to 12 minutes. Remove the baking sheet from the oven and let the packages rest for 1 minute to let the heat subside.

NUTRITIONAL
INFORMATION PER
SERVING

Total Calories: 295

Total Fat: 11 gm.

Saturated Fat: 2 gm.

Cholesterol: 94 mg.

Sodium: 82 mg.

Fiber Rating: 0.5 gm.

To serve, place the packages on individual plates and bring to the table. With a sharp knife, cut a slit in the top of each package at the table, taking care not to burn yourself on the steam as it escapes. Fold the paper back to reveal the salmon and vegetables, leaving them on the parchment paper.

NOTE: Cooking en papillote is a particularly healthy cooking method because the nutrients are locked into the package as the food cooks and you don't have to rely on fat to keep the food moist. You can prepare these packets ahead, refrigerate them, and cook them when you're ready.

Pan-Roasted Pheasant Breast with Braised Apples and Cabbage

From Roman times and throughout the medieval era, pheasant was regarded as a culinary indulgence, and its presentation at the table was lavish. While the plumage of the male pheasant is more brilliant, the hen provides juicier, more tender meat. Connoisseurs of poultry and game are unanimous in calling pheasant the finest-flavored bird of all, and it is also the leanest. Because of its low fat content, pheasant can dry out and become stringy if it is overcooked, but roasting it with other ingredients, as in this recipe, ensures that the meat remains moist. This is a great holiday dish with a difference.

SERVES: 4

4 skinless pheasant breasts, about 5 ounces, each with the drumstick section of the wing bone intact

1 tablespoon minced garlic

1 teaspoon freshly cracked black pepper

1 tablespoon olive oil

4 cups peeled, cored, seeded, and finely diced Red Delicious apples

$^1/_4$ cup raisins

$^1/_4$ cup golden raisins

2 cups sliced white cabbage

2 cups sliced red cabbage

$1^1/_2$ cups apple juice

$^1/_4$ cup honey

1 tablespoon ground cinnamon

1 tablespoon ground cloves

Pinch of ground mace

4 sprigs rosemary, for garnish

Preheat the oven to 375°.

Remove the meat from the drumstick section of the wing bone and reserve for stock or another use ("frenching" the bone in this way is done for purposes of presentation). Rub the pheasant breasts with the garlic and pepper. Heat the olive oil in a nonstick sauté pan. When the pan is hot, add the pheasant and sear over medium-high heat for 3 to 4 minutes per side, until golden brown. Be careful; the garlic will burn if the heat is too high. Remove the breasts from the pan and set aside.

Thoroughly mix together all the remaining ingredients in a mixing bowl and transfer to a small roasting pan. Place the pheasant breasts on top. Roast in the oven for 10 to 12 minutes, until the breasts are cooked through.

To serve, slice the pheasant breasts thinly. Spoon the apple and cabbage mixture in a strip running down the center of each serving plate from top to bottom. Fan out the pheasant slices on top of the apple and cabbage mixture. Spoon the juices from the pan around and garnish the pheasant with the rosemary. Serve immediately.

NUTRITIONAL
INFORMATION PER
SERVING

Total Calories: 450

Total Fat: 9 gm.

Saturated Fat: 2 gm.

Cholesterol: 70 mg.

Sodium: 66 mg.

Fiber Rating: 5 gm.

Beef Medallions with Port and Sweet Onion Sauce and Potato-Leek Pierogis

SERVES: 4

Beef, port, and sweet onions make a classic, richly flavored combination. Pierogis are half-moon-shaped dumplings of Polish heritage. They usually contain potatoes and other vegetables, and sometimes they contain minced pork, cabbage, or cheese. Pierogis are usually served as a side dish, but they are also often sautéed in butter and served as an appetizer or snack. Buy the pasta sheets or make the ravioli dough recipe on page 14. This is a hearty, filling dish, so make it the main meal and eat lightly the rest of the day.

PIEROGIS

2 baking potatoes (about 14 ounces), peeled and coarsely chopped

1 teaspoon olive oil

1$^{1}/_{2}$ tablespoons minced garlic

1 cup thinly sliced leeks, white part only

$^{1}/_{2}$ cup thinly sliced and stemmed shiitake mushrooms

1 tablespoon minced fresh thyme

1 tablespoon minced fresh rosemary

1 tablespoon unseasoned rice wine vinegar

Freshly cracked black pepper to taste

2 fresh pasta sheets, about 8$^{1}/_{2}$ inches by 12 inches

1 egg white, lightly beaten

PORT AND SWEET ONION SAUCE

1 teaspoon olive oil

1 large Vidalia or other sweet onion, sliced

1 tablespoon minced garlic

$^{3}/_{4}$ cup dry port

1$^{1}/_{2}$ cups Low-Sodium Beef Broth (page 226)

$^{1}/_{2}$ tablespoon minced fresh thyme

$^{1}/_{2}$ tablespoon minced fresh rosemary

1 tablespoon cornstarch

1 tablespoon cold water

BEEF

1 teaspoon olive oil

8 beef tenderloin medallions, about 3 ounces each

GARNISH:

1 carrot, peeled and finely julienned

1 red bell pepper, seeded and finely julienned

1 scallion, white part only, finely julienned

4 rosemary sprigs

To prepare the pierogis, bring a saucepan of salted water to a boil and add the potatoes. Turn down the heat and cook at a low boil for 12 to 15 minutes, until soft. Drain the potatoes, place in a mixing bowl, and beat with a heavy duty electric mixer (or by hand) until smooth. Set aside.

Heat the olive oil in a nonstick sauté pan. Add the garlic, leeks, and mushrooms, and sauté over medium heat for 2 to 3 minutes. Stir the leek mixture into the mashed potatoes, mixing thoroughly. Stir in the thyme, rosemary, vinegar, and pepper, and set aside.

Lay out the pasta sheets on a work surface and, using a 4-inch round cutter, cut out 12 circles of pasta. Brush the egg white in a $1/2$-inch strip along the edge of each pasta round. Place about 1 tablespoon of the potato filling on each round and fold over in a half-moon shape. Gently seal the edges together with your fingers, removing all the air from each pierogi. Set aside.

To prepare the sauce, heat the olive oil in a saucepan. Add the onion and garlic and sweat over medium heat for 2 to 3 minutes. Deglaze the pan with the port. Add the broth, thyme, and rosemary, and bring to a boil. Mix together the cornstarch and water in a cup and stir into the sauce until the mixture thickens. Keep warm.

Bring a saucepan of water to a boil. Add the pierogis and cook at a low boil for about 5 minutes. Remove from the water with a slotted spoon and drain thoroughly. Toss with the sauce in the pan.

NUTRITIONAL INFORMATION PER SERVING

Total Calories: 550

Total Fat: 14 gm.

Saturated Fat: 5 gm.

Cholesterol: 121 mg.

Sodium: 101 mg.

Fiber Rating: 2 gm.

To prepare the beef medallions, heat the olive oil in a large sauté pan. When the pan is hot, add the medallions and sear over high heat for 1¹/₂ to 2 minutes per side, or until browned and to the desired doneness.

To serve, arrange 3 pierogis together at the top of each serving plate and lean the beef medallions against the pierogis. Ladle the sauce at the bottom of each plate and garnish the top of the medallions with the julienned vegetable garnish and rosemary sprigs. Serve immediately.

NOTE: The pierogis contain 215 calories per serving, with 2 grams of fat, 1 gram of unsaturated fat, 26 milligrams of sodium, 1 gram of fiber, and no cholesterol. The sauce has 92 calories per serving with 1 gram of fat and 3 grams of sodium.

Pear and Pistachio Strudel with Oregano-Almond Crust

Strudel, a traditional Bavarian rolled pastry usually filled with fruit or cheese and a streusel (crumb) mixture, is always a safe bet as a winter dessert. Classic strudel recipes contain plenty of butter, but this one is a proud exception. The most common type of strudel filling consists of apple and raisins, but my favorite is pears and pistachios, which make a wonderful flavor combination. (Plums and pistachios are almost as good!)

SERVES: 6

FILLING

³/₄ cup sugar

2 ¹/₂ tablespoons cornstarch

6 pears, peeled, cored, and diced

¹/₄ cup chopped pistachios

CRUST

¹/₄ cup finely ground almonds

2 tablespoons sugar

2 tablespoons minced fresh oregano

8 sheets phyllo dough

2 teaspoons sugar

Pinch of ground cinnamon

Preheat the oven to 350°.

To prepare the filling, thoroughly mix together the sugar and cornstarch in a mixing bowl. Stir in the pears and pistachios, and set aside.

To prepare the crust, combine the almonds, sugar, and oregano in a separate mixing bowl and set aside. Place a clean kitchen towel, about double the size of the phyllo sheets, on a flat surface (the towel will help you start rolling the phyllo without tearing it). Place 2 phyllo sheets stacked on top of each other at the top of the towel and place 2 stacked phyllo sheets below the first, slightly overlapping the top stack by about 2 inches. Brush the exposed phyllo with a little water and sprinkle with half of the crust mixture. Layer the remaining phyllo sheets on top of the original layers, in the same manner. Brush the exposed phyllo with a little water and sprinkle with the remaining crust mixture.

Spoon the filling in a strip along the top portion of the phyllo and roll up the strudel toward you, as tightly as possible, using the towel to begin rolling evenly (once you have started rolling the strudel, remove the towel). Transfer the strudel to a baking sheet coated with nonstick cooking spray. Spray the top of the strudel with butter-flavored vegetable spray. Mix together the sugar and cinnamon, and sprinkle over the strudel. Bake in the oven for about 40 minutes, or until golden brown. Serve warm.

NOTE: This is another dessert recipe that contains herbs. Adding herbs enhances the flavors and allows the amounts of less healthy ingredients such as butter, cream, and sugar to be reduced. Phyllo dough is a wonderful substitute for traditional pastry dough; it can be used in sweet or savory recipes with great success.

NUTRITIONAL
INFORMATION PER
SERVING

Total Calories: 344

Total Fat: 7 gm.

Saturated Fat: 1 gm.

Cholesterol: 107 mg.

Sodium: 2 mg.

Fiber Rating: 5 gm.

Banana-Anise Tofulato Sundae
with Black Walnut Praline
and Cocoa Glaze

SERVES: 4

Our guests invariably ask about tofulato, which we explain is like gelato, only made with tofu, or soy bean curd. A winter sundae like this one brings back welcome thoughts of summer, no matter what the temperature outside. The tofu has a custardlike consistency and a remarkable capacity to take on other flavors. In this recipe, it makes a great medium for the flavors of banana and anise. This recipe features a variety of textures and temperatures, which can be further accentuated by serving the perfect accompaniment: a cup of steaming espresso with a twist of lemon.

TOFULATO SUNDAE

3 ripe bananas

1 package silken tofu (10 $^1/_4$ ounces)

2 tablespoons freshly squeezed orange juice

2 tablespoons ground anise seed

$^1/_2$ vanilla bean, split in half lengthwise and seeds scraped out

PRALINE

1 egg white

2 tablespoons sugar

$^3/_4$ cup finely chopped black walnuts (or regular walnuts)

GLAZE

$^1/_4$ cup sugar

$^1/_2$ tablespoon cornstarch

1 tablespoon unsweetened cocoa

$^1/_3$ cup cold water

2 tablespoons evaporated nonfat milk

Preheat the oven to 350°.

To prepare the tofulato, place the bananas, tofu, orange juice, anise, and vanilla bean seeds in a food processor or blender and purée until smooth. Transfer the mixture to the tub of an ice-cream maker and freeze according to the manufacturer's directions.

To prepare the praline, whisk together the egg white and sugar in a mixing bowl until foamy. Stir in the walnuts. Spread the mixture out on a baking sheet coated with nonstick cooking spray. Transfer to the oven and bake for 20 minutes, or until golden brown. Remove from the oven and let cool. Break into large pieces and set aside.

To prepare the glaze, thoroughly mix together the sugar, cornstarch, cocoa, and water in a saucepan. Cook over medium heat, stirring occasionally, until thickened. Remove from the heat and stir in the evaporated milk. Set aside.

To serve, place 2 scoops of the tofulato in the bottom of a tall sundae glass. Top with a layer of the praline and then a layer of the glaze. Repeat the layers until the glass is full. Serve with an iced tea spoon.

❧

NOTES: Tofu, which is made from soy beans, is no longer regarded as a food for health nuts—it has entered the mainstream and is a wonderful source of protein and beneficial amino acids. Silken tofu is a particularly smooth style of tofu that you will find in the refrigerated section in health food stores and some supermarkets. It can also be used for soups, sauces, and dressings.

Gelatin prevents the components in tofulato from separating while stored in the freezer. If you wish to freeze the dessert, mix 2 teaspoons gelatin with $^1/_4$ cup warm water, stir to dissolve, and add to the tofulato recipe before freezing.

NUTRITIONAL
INFORMATION PER
SERVING

Total Calories: 243

Total Fat: 6 gm.

Saturated Fat: 0.4 gm.

Cholesterol: 0.3 mg.

Sodium: 30 mg.

Fiber Rating: 3 gm.

Upside-Down Caribbean Mango Gingerbread

SERVES: 6

This recipe is something special—the first time I tried it, I couldn't believe how good it tasted. In this brainchild of Eric Boerner, our former pastry chef, the classic gingerbread is combined with an upside-down cake. The most common type of upside-down cake is made with pineapple, but here, we make use of the seasonal mangoes that come from the Caribbean in the middle of winter to remind us of the balmy tropics. So cut a slice of this cake, pass a cup of mulled cider, and pretend you're on a sun-drenched, palm-fringed beach.

BATTER

$1/4$ cup sugar

2 tablespoons dark molasses

$1/4$ cup egg substitute (such as Eggbeaters)

2 tablespoons nonfat milk powder

$1/4$ cup water

$1/4$ cup fat-free margarine, melted and cooled

$1/4$ cup pitted and puréed prunes

$1/2$ teaspoon pure vanilla extract

$2/3$ cup all-purpose flour

2 teaspoons baking powder

$1/2$ teaspoon powdered ginger

$1/4$ teaspoon ground cardamom

$1/2$ teaspoon ground coriander

MANGO TOPPING

$1/3$ cup brown sugar

2 tablespoons fat-free margarine

$1/4$ cup Karo syrup

1 mango, peeled, pitted, and sliced

Preheat the oven to 350°.

To prepare the topping, thoroughly mix together the brown sugar, margarine, and Karo syrup in a mixing bowl. Spread the mixture in the bottom of an 8-inch cake pan sprayed with nonstick cooking spray. Arrange the mango slices on top and set aside.

To prepare the batter, combine the sugar, molasses, and egg substitute in the bowl of a heavy duty electric mixer and beat on medium speed for 5 minutes. Thoroughly mix together the milk powder and water in a mixing bowl until dissolved, and add to the bowl of the mixer. Separately blend together the margarine, prunes, and vanilla extract. Sift together the flour, baking powder, ginger, cardamom, and coriander in a mixing bowl. In alternate increments, add the molasses and prune mixtures to form a batter. Carefully pour the batter into the cake pan on top of the mangoes and transfer to the oven. Bake for 30 minutes.

Remove the pan from the oven and let cool slightly. Invert onto a serving platter, and cut into slices.

NUTRITIONAL
INFORMATION PER
SERVING

Total Calories: 236

Total Fat: 1 gm.

Saturated Fat: 0.2 gm.

Cholesterol: 0.3 mg.

Sodium: 260 mg.

Fiber Rating: 2 gm.

Baked Apples Stuffed with Indian Pudding and Stewed Apricots

SERVES: 6

Baked apples are a staple of the American dessert pantry, and typical of central Pennsylvania, especially in Amish and Pennsylvania Dutch country. Indian Pudding is a traditional, filling dessert from New England; this lighter version omits the usual eggs and molasses. Used as a stuffing, the pudding provides a crunchy texture and makes an excellent backdrop for the sweet, fermented flavor of the stewed apricots. This is one dish that tastes great reheated straight from the microwave.

STEWED APRICOTS

2 cups dry white wine, such as
   Chardonnay

$1/3$ cup sugar

1 cinnamon stick

3 cloves

$2/3$ cup diced dried apricots (preferably
   unsulphured)

APPLES

Juice of 2 freshly squeezed lemons

2 tablespoons sugar

6 Rome Beauty or Red Delicious
   apples, peeled and cored

INDIAN PUDDING

$1^1/4$ cups nonfat milk

1 tablespoon sugar

$1/2$ vanilla bean, split in half lengthwise and seeds scraped out

$1/4$ cup cornmeal

Minced zest of $1/2$ orange

$1/4$ teaspoon almond extract

To prepare the stewed apricots, combine the wine, sugar, cinnamon, and cloves in a small saucepan and bring to a simmer. Stir in the apricots and cook for 15 to 20 minutes, until tender. Set aside.

To prepare the apples, mix together the lemon juice and sugar in a mixing bowl. Cut small slice off the bottoms of the apples so they will sit level. Place the apples in a shallow baking dish, sliced side down, and brush with the lemon-sugar mixture. Set aside.

Preheat the oven to 350°.

To prepare the pudding, combine the milk, sugar, and vanilla seeds in a heavy-bottomed saucepan and bring to a boil. Stir in the cornmeal, zest, and almond extract, and cook over medium heat for 6 to 8 minutes, stirring constantly with a wooden spoon, until the mixture thickens. Stir in half of the stewed apricots and remove the pan from the heat. Spoon the pudding into the middle of the apples (serve leftover pudding the next day with ice cream).

Pour the remaining stewed apricots into the bottom of the baking dish. Cover the dish with aluminum foil and poke 5 or 6 holes in the foil to let the steam escape. Transfer to the oven and bake for 20 to 25 minutes, until the apples are soft.

Remove the pan from the oven and, using a spatula, carefully transfer the apples to a shallow serving bowl. Spoon the stewed apricots and cooking liquid around each apple, and serve immediately.

❧

NOTE: It is important to use wooden spoons when stirring ingredients in a metal saucepan or bowl. Metal-on-metal contact may lead to microscopic metal particles being incorporated into your food. Aluminum pots and spoons especially should be avoided.

NUTRITIONAL INFORMATION PER SERVING
Total Calories: 267
Total Fat: 1 gm.
Saturated Fat: 0.4 gm.
Cholesterol: 2 mg.
Sodium: 33 mg.
Fiber Rating: 4 gm.

Holidays

Married-Ten-Years Purse with Oysters, Spinach, and Tomato Coulis / 192
Bouquet Salad with Edible Flowers and Champagne Vinaigrette / 194
Petit Filet with Lobster, Brown Rice, Red Peppers, and Roasted Vegetables / 195
Chocolate Profiteroles with Tarragon-Fig Marmalade and Cinnamon-Honey Caramel / 198

☙ MOTHER'S DAY ❧

Roasted Red Bell Pepper Soup with Cilantro Cream / 201
Oriental Smoked Trout, Endive, and Bamboo Shoot Salad / 203
Anise-Rubbed Roasted Chicken with Braised Fennel and Mushroom Couscous / 205
Creamy Lemon-Yogurt Mousse / 208

☙ FOURTH OF JULY ❧

Roasted Baby New Potato Salad / 210
English Cucumber and Red Onion Slaw / 211
Barbecued Spice-Rubbed Chicken with Chickeria Barbecue Sauce / 212
Blackberry Shortcake with Minted Orange Chantilly and Cilantro Oil / 214

☙ THANKSGIVING / CHRISTMAS ❧

Three-Fish Chowder / 217
Haricots Verts and Balsamic-Glazed Salad / 219
Herb-Rubbed Holiday Turkey with Creamy Polenta and Steamed Asparagus / 220
Red Yam Corn Cake with Pumpkin Mousse / 222

Opposite: Valentines Day

Married-Ten-Years Purse with Oysters, Spinach, and Tomato Coulis

SERVES: 4

The presentlike purse, the aphrodisiac reputation of the oysters, and the Valentine's red of the coulis all add to the spirit of this special dish. And speaking of marriage, if ever two flavors and textures were suited to each other, it's spinach and oysters, which share a subtle, ironlike taste and a soft, smooth texture. It's important not to overcook either one. Use large oysters for this recipe because they tend to cook better than smaller ones and you don't want them to dry out. I prefer domestic varieties from the West Coast such as Westcott Bay or Washington oysters.

TOMATO COULIS

2 cups diced tomatoes

$^1/_4$ cup Low-Sodium Chicken Stock (page 225)

1 teaspoon minced garlic

1 teaspoon minced shallots

1 tablespoon chopped fresh dill

Pinch of freshly ground black pepper

PURSE

8 freshly shucked oysters, liquor reserved

1 teaspoon olive oil

$1^1/_2$ tablespoons minced garlic

$1^1/_2$ tablespoons minced shallots

$^1/_2$ cup fresh spinach

1 teaspoon chopped fresh dill

Freshly ground black pepper to taste

4 sheets phyllo dough

Combine all of the coulis ingredients in a small saucepan and bring to a simmer over low heat. Continue cooking the mixture over low heat for 15 to 20 minutes. Remove the pan from the heat, transfer the mixture to a food processor or blender, and purée until very smooth. Strain the mixture through a fine sieve into a bowl, set aside, and keep warm.

To prepare the purses, heat a nonstick sauté pan, add the oysters, and quickly sauté for about 2 minutes over medium heat. Remove the oysters from the pan and reserve. Add the olive oil, garlic, shallots, spinach, and oyster liquor to the pan and quickly sauté over medium heat for 1 to 2 minutes, until the spinach has wilted. Transfer the spinach mixture to a bowl and fold in the dill and black pepper. Set aside to cool.

Preheat the oven to 425°.

Lay out a sheet of phyllo dough on a work surface and lightly brush with water. Top with another phyllo sheet, brush with water, and repeat for the remaining phyllo sheets, stacking them as you go. Cut the stacked phyllo into 4 equal squares. Divide the spinach mixture between the middle of the phyllo squares and place 2 oysters on top of each portion of spinach. Bring the corners of each square inwards, meeting in the center, and then pinch the dough together to seal tightly. Transfer the phyllo purses to a nonstick baking sheet and bake in the oven for 5 to 7 minutes, or until golden brown.

To serve, ladle the warm coulis in the center of each serving plate and place the purses in the center of the coulis.

NOTE: When selecting oysters, buy only those with tightly closed shells or whose shells close when tapped. If you buy shucked oysters, be sure they are plump, cream colored, and packed in clear, not milky, liquid; the liquid should account for less than 10 percent of their weight. Although oysters vary in size, flavor, texture, and sodium content, 3 ounces of raw oysters contain on average 59 calories, 6 grams of protein, 2 grams of fat, 47 milligrams of cholesterol, and 95 milligrams of sodium.

NUTRITIONAL
INFORMATION PER
SERVING

Total Calories: 109

Total Fat: 3 gm.

Saturated Fat: 0.4 gm.

Cholesterol: 97 mg.

Sodium: 236 mg.

Fiber Rating: 1 gm.

Bouquet Salad with Edible Flowers and Champagne Vinaigrette

What more appropriate way to celebrate a Valentine's Day meal than with flowers? The salad will look like a bouquet if you use a variety of colored edible flowers—very romantic! I grow a variety of edible flowers indoors at home for such purposes. The Champagne vinaigrette is another celebratory touch that's ideal for the light and colorful salad and a perfect match with a Valentine's Day Champagne toast.

SERVES: 4

NUTRITIONAL INFORMATION PER SERVING

Total Calories: 47

Total Fat: 2.2 gm.

Saturated Fat: 0.3 gm.

Cholesterol: 0 mg.

Sodium: 15 mg.

Fiber Rating: 2.4 gm.

CHAMPAGNE VINAIGRETTE

$1/2$ teaspoon finely minced garlic

1 teaspoon minced shallots

1 tablespoon Champagne vinegar

3 tablespoons Low-Sodium Chicken Stock (page 225)

$1/4$ teaspoon freshly squeezed lime juice

$1/4$ teaspoon sugar

Pinch of freshly ground white pepper

1 $1/2$ teaspoons olive oil

1 tablespoon minced fresh parsley

SALAD

4 ounces mixed baby greens such as mâche, frisée, radicchio, and baby red oak lettuce

16 to 20 small edible flowers such as nasturtiums, marigolds, pansies, and chive flowers, for garnish

To prepare the vinaigrette, whisk together the garlic, shallots, vinegar, stock, lime juice, sugar, and white pepper in a small mixing bowl until well blended. Slowly whisk in the olive oil, whisking constantly, until emulsified. Stir in the parsley. Place the greens in a mixing bowl and toss with the vinaigrette. Place a mound of the lettuce in the center of each serving plate and garnish with 4 or 5 of the flowers around each plate.

Petit Filet with Lobster, Brown Rice, Red Peppers, and Roasted Vegetables

SERVES: 4

This recipe combines two of the most popular Valentine's Day menu items—beef filet and lobster. This is a decadently rich but delightful combination. If you can't splurge on this special day, then when can you? This dish adapts the classic carpetbag steak recipe that was created in mid-nineteenth- century San Francisco during the days of the gold rush and has remained popular ever since. Named after the bulging item of luggage, the steak was stuffed with oysters, which were far more plentiful back then than now. Steaks can be stuffed with all kinds of ingredients, but it's important that the stuffing be precooked; otherwise, by the time it cooks, the meat will be incinerated! The roasted red bell peppers provide the Valentine's Day color. The long-grain brown rice is not as starchy as its short-grain counterpart, and it's healthier than white rice. Note that the brown rice should be soaked for at least two hours, and preferably overnight, before cooking.

ROASTED VEGETABLES

1 head garlic

2 carrots (about 8 ounces), peeled and cut into $1^{1}/_{2}$ inch slices

1 red onion, sliced

2 tablespoons unseasoned rice wine vinegar

1 tablespoon olive oil

Freshly ground black pepper to taste

FILETS AND LOBSTER TAILS

4 lobster tails, about 2 ounces each

4 center-cut beef filets, about 4 ounces each

1 tablespoon finely minced garlic

1 teaspoon chopped fresh dill

Freshly ground black pepper to taste

RICE

$1/2$ cups long-grain brown rice

1 teaspoon olive oil

1 onion, minced

2 cloves garlic, minced

3 cups Low-Sodium Chicken Stock
(page 225)

1 tablespoon ground cumin

Freshly ground black pepper to taste

$1/4$ cup seeded and finely diced red
bell pepper

1 tablespoon chopped fresh tarragon

1 tablespoon chopped fresh parsley

Soak the rice in water for at least 2 hours, and preferably overnight.

Preheat the oven to 400°.

To prepare the vegetables, wrap the garlic in aluminum foil and roast in the oven for about 30 minutes. Remove from the oven and let cool. Squeeze the garlic from the bulb by firmly pressing on it from the bottom. Set the soft garlic aside.

Place the carrots and onions in a roasting pan and toss with the vinegar and olive oil to coat evenly. Transfer to the oven and roast for about 1 hour, tossing every 15 minutes. Stir in the garlic for the last 15 minutes of cooking time. Remove the vegetables from the oven and season with the black pepper. Let cool to room temperature. (Leave the oven set to 400° as you'll need it again.)

Drain and rinse the rice under cold water until the water runs clear. Heat a saucepan coated with nonstick cooking spray, add the olive oil, onions, and garlic, and sauté over medium-high heat for 2 to 3 minutes, until the mixture turns a light golden brown. Add the rice and stock and bring the mixture to a boil. Stir in the cumin and black pepper, reduce the heat to low, cover, and cook for about 20 minutes, until the rice is tender and all of the stock has been absorbed. Remove the pan from the heat and stir in the bell peppers, tarragon, and parsley. Keep warm.

Place the lobster tails on skewers to prevent them from curling during the cooking process. Bring a saucepan of water fitted with a steamer basket to a boil. Place the lobster tails in the steamer basket and cook for 4 or 5 minutes, until cooked through. Remove from the steamer and let cool. Remove the lobster meat from the shell, discarding the shell.

Using a sharp boning or paring knife, cut a pocket in the center of each filet just large enough to fit the lobster. Season each of the lobster tails with the garlic, dill and black pepper. Stuff one tail into each filet.

Heat a nonstick sauté pan coated with nonstick cooking spray. Add the filets to the hot pan and sear over high heat for 2 to 3 minutes on each side. Transfer the seared fillets to a rack placed on a baking sheet and finish in the oven for about 4 to 5 minutes for medium-rare. Transfer the stuffed filets to serving plates and serve with the rice and vegetables.

NOTES: Lobster was so plentiful in the 1800s that it was used as bait for cod and bass! Lobster has no saturated fat, so in moderation it is acceptable as part of a low-fat, low-cholesterol diet.

Ounce for ounce, brown rice has double the iron found in white rice, three times the fiber, niacin, and Vitamin B6, and five times more thiamin and vitamin E. Presoaking brown rice cuts the cooking time in half.

NUTRITIONAL
INFORMATION PER
SERVING

Total Calories: 406

Total Fat: 13 gm.

Saturated Fat: 4 gm.

Cholesterol: 105 mg.

Sodium: 291 mg.

Fiber Rating: 3 gm

Chocolate Profiteroles with Tarragon-Fig Marmalade and Cinnamon-Honey Caramel

SERVES: 6

*P*rofiteroles are a local tradition in Philadelphia that we just could not leave out of this book, least of all for that celebration of chocolate known as Valentine's Day! We serve various other types of these cream puffs at the Rittenhouse—banana cream and chocolate, and chocolate sauce with ginger ice cream—but these chocolate-flavored profiteroles filled with sweetened cheese and fig marmalade, perfected by Philadelphia pastry chef Eric Boerner, are my favorite. It's probably because I love figs so much, and the aromatic contrast provided by the tarragon takes them into the realm of the sublime. This recipe provides a lowfat approach to a classic.

PROFITEROLE BATTER

$^1/_2$ cup all-purpose flour

1 tablespoon unsweetened cocoa

$^1/_4$ cup soft corn oil margarine

$^1/_2$ cup water

$^1/_2$ cup egg substitute (such as Eggbeaters), plus 2 egg whites

PROFITEROLE FILLING

$1^1/_2$ cups nonfat ricotta cheese

2 tablespoons cocoa

$^1/_4$ cup superfine sugar

MARMALADE

$1^1/_4$ cups brewed black tea

2 tablespoons freshly squeezed orange juice

6 to 8 dried figs (about $^3/_4$ cup)

$^1/_4$ cup loosely packed fresh tarragon leaves

CARAMEL

$^1/_2$ cup honey

2 tablespoons brown sugar

$^2/_3$ cup brewed black tea

1 tablespoon corn oil margarine

1 teaspoon cocoa

$^1/_4$ teaspoon ground cinnamon

Preheat the oven to 400°.

To prepare the batter, thoroughly combine the flour and cocoa in a mixing bowl. Combine the margarine and water in a small saucepan and bring to a boil. Stir in the cocoa and flour mixture and cook for 5 to 7 minutes, stirring constantly, until the mixture forms a ball of chocolate paste. Transfer to the bowl of a heavy duty electric mixer and beat on medium speed until the mixture cools slightly and is no longer steaming. With the machine still running, slowly add the egg substitute and egg white, scraping the sides of the bowl down occasionally, and beat until incorporated.

Drop about 16 rounded tablespoons of the batter onto a nonstick baking sheet coated with nonstick cooking spray, leaving a space about the size of the batter between each one. Transfer to the oven and bake for 25 minutes, or until puffy and dry. Remove from the oven and let cool.

Combine all the filling ingredients in a food processor and purée until smooth. Set aside.

To prepare the marmalade, combine the tea and orange juice in a saucepan and bring to a boil. Add the figs, cover, and remove from the heat. Set aside for 10 minutes, or until the figs are soft. Transfer the mixture to a food processor, add the tarragon, and purée until smooth. Set aside.

To prepare the caramel, combine the honey and sugar in a sauté pan and caramelize over high heat for 2 to 3 minutes. Remove from the heat and stir in the tea, margarine, cocoa, and cinnamon. If any lumps remain, briefly return the pan to medium heat and stir until the lumps dissolve. Keep warm.

Slice the profiteroles in half horizontally, all the way through. Spoon 1 tablespoon of the filling on the bottom half, and top with 1 teaspoon of the marmalade. Top with the other half of the profiterole. To serve, place 2 profiteroles on each serving plate and drizzle with the warm caramel.

NUTRITIONAL INFORMATION PER SERVING
Total Calories: 260
Total Fat: 7 gm.
Saturated Fat: 1 gm.
Cholesterol: 0.2 mg.
Sodium: 201 mg.
Fiber Rating: 2 gm.

Roasted Red Pepper Soup with Cilantro Cream

I created this dish for my wife Candy, the best mother I know! Roasted red bell peppers and cilantro are two of her all-time favorite ingredients, so what better reason to create this soup for her. This soup can just as successfully be served chilled; it takes on such a different character that it's like a whole new soup. Double the recipe and keep the extra in the refrigerator. A glance at the recipe may suggest that there's enough garlic in the recipe to keep vampires at bay well into the future, but it matches the red bell peppers so well. The cilantro cream is best prepared ahead (at least 1 hour and preferably a day ahead, to let the flavors marry), and its intense green color contrasts strikingly with the red soup. Since the "cream" in the cilantro cream comes from the very low-calorie nonfat yogurt, this soup is a calorie/taste bargain!

SERVES: 4

CILANTRO CREAM

¹/₄ cup nonfat yogurt

1¹/₂ tablespoons minced cilantro

¹/₄ teaspoon freshly squeezed lime juice

¹/₄ teaspoon sugar

Pinch of freshly ground white pepper

SOUP

¹/₄ cup chopped red onions

¹/₄ cup coarsely chopped fennel bulb

2 tablespoons chopped garlic

11 red bell peppers, roasted, peeled, seeded, and coarsely chopped (page 231)

3 cups Low-Sodium Chicken Stock (page 225)

¹/₄ cup loosely packed chopped fresh basil

¹/₄ teaspoon freshly cracked black pepper

4 sprigs cilantro, for garnish

Place all the ingredients for the cilantro cream in a food processor and purée until smooth. Refrigerate until needed.

To prepare the soup, heat a saucepan coated with nonstick cooking spray. Add the onions, fennel, and garlic, and sauté over medium-high heat for 2 minutes; do not let it burn. Add the bell peppers and stock, and bring to a boil. Reduce the heat to low and simmer for 15 to 20 minutes. Stir in the basil and black pepper. Transfer the mixture to a blender or food processor and purée until smooth. If the soup is too thick, add a little more stock.

To serve, ladle the soup into serving bowls and drizzle with the cilantro cream. Garnish with the cilantro sprigs.

NOTES: Red bell peppers are actually ripe green peppers; they are high in vitamins A and C and have more of these vitamins than green peppers. Red bell peppers have about 22 calories each and a good amount of fiber.

NUTRITIONAL INFORMATION PER SERVING

Total Calories: 73

Total Fat: 1 gm.

Saturated Fat: 0 gm.

Cholesterol: 0 mg.

Sodium: 24 mg.

Fiber Rating: 2 gm.

Oriental Smoked Trout, Endive, and Bamboo Shoot Salad

*N*ow here's an interesting combination of ingredients. Smoked trout, redolent of campfires and the great American outdoors, Belgian endive and radicchio, which lend an elegant and distinctively European touch, and the Asian influence of mirin, bamboo shoots, and lemongrass. It's a cross-cultural combination that really works. Lemongrass has a unique flavor and is essential for many Thai and Vietnamese dishes, but because it's not always available, I encourage people to grow it in a windowbox or in the garden, which is what I do. But be careful—it can grow like a weed and take over before you know it. When buying radicchio, make sure the leaves will work well as cups to hold the salad.

SERVES: 4

TROUT MIXTURE

8 ounces skinless, boneless smoked trout

8 canned bamboo shoots, rinsed and finely chopped

8 Belgian endive leaves, finely chopped

$1/4$ red bell pepper, seeded and finely diced

$1/4$ green bell pepper, seeded and finely diced

1 shallot, finely diced

$1/4$ cup mirin

2 tablespoons finely minced lemongrass

1 teaspoon minced garlic

$1/2$ tablespoon coarsely chopped cilantro

SALAD

24 Belgian endive leaves

24 canned bamboo shoots, rinsed and julienned

4 large Bibb lettuce leaves

4 radicchio leaves, shaped like cups

4 cilantro sprigs, for garnish

NUTRITIONAL
INFORMATION PER
SERVING

Total Calories: 81

Total Fat: 2 gm.

Saturated Fat: 0.4 gm.

Cholesterol: 32 mg.

Sodium: 451 mg.

Fiber Rating: 1 gm.

Flake the trout with a fork and place in a mixing bowl. Thoroughly combine the remaining ingredients for the trout mixture in a mixing bowl and refrigerate for 2 to 4 hours.

Arrange 6 of the endive leaves around each plate in a flower shape (like petals). Place a sliced bamboo shoot in the center of each endive leaf. Place the Bibb lettuce at the apex of the endive leaves in the middle of the plate and top with a radicchio leaf cup. Spoon the trout mixture in the radicchio cups and garnish with the cilantro sprigs.

NOTE: Mirin, also known as rice wine, is a golden, sweet, low-alcohol wine made from rice. It's a staple in the Japanese kitchen, used primarily to enhance other flavors rather than for its own characteristics.

Anise-Rubbed Roasted Chicken with Braised Fennel and Mushroom Couscous

This is a dish that will impress and delight any mother, as we have discovered at the Rittenhouse. The aromatic and rather exotic ingredients work together well. Toasting the spices used for the rub intensifies their flavor and gives them a pleasing complexity, and the rub in turn enhances the chicken's natural flavor. The rub also matches the delicate, faintly licoricelike fennel, and it can be used with equal success with most types of poultry. Use free-range chicken whenever you can—it's not only healthier for you, but it definitely has a cleaner, more distinctive flavor than mass-produced chicken. For the couscous, you can substitute rehydrated dried shiitake mushrooms for the fresh shiitakes, and, in a pinch, button mushrooms will do.

CHICKEN

2 teaspoons anise seeds

1 teaspoon fennel seeds

1 teaspoon coriander seeds

10 black peppercorns

1 teaspoon olive oil

2 teaspoons finely minced garlic

2 free-range chickens, about 2 pounds each, skin removed

BRAISED FENNEL

1 tablespoon minced garlic

1 tablespoon thinly sliced red onions

2 fennel bulbs, cut finely into $1/8$-inch-thick slices

2 cups Low-Sodium Chicken Stock (page 225)

$1/4$ cup rice wine vinegar

1 teaspoon sugar

Pinch of freshly ground white pepper

1 tomato, blanched, peeled, seeded, and julienned

2 tablespoons chopped fresh parsley

MUSHROOM COUSCOUS

1^1/$_2$ tablespoons minced garlic

^{1}/$_2$ cup finely chopped onions

^{3}/$_4$ cup chopped cremini mushrooms or shiitake mushrooms

^{3}/$_4$ cup chopped oyster mushrooms

1 cup chopped shiitake mushrooms

2^1/$_2$ cups Low-Sodium Chicken Stock (page 225)

^{1}/$_4$ teaspoon minced fresh thyme

^{1}/$_4$ cup chopped fresh parsley

2 tablespoons minced fresh dill

1 box (10 ounces) couscous

Preheat the oven to 375°.

To prepare the chicken, place the anise, fennel, coriander, and peppercorns in a small nonstick sauté pan or dry heavy skillet. Toast over medium-low heat, shaking the pan occasionally, for 2 to 3 minutes, until fragrant. Transfer to a spice grinder and grind to a powder. Place in a mixing bowl, add the olive oil and garlic, and thoroughly combine. Rub the chickens with the spice rub until thoroughly covered. Place the chickens in a roasting pan, and wrap securely with aluminum foil. Transfer to the oven and roast for 35 minutes. Remove the foil, increase the heat to 425°, and cook for 15 minutes longer, or until lightly browned and cooked through. Remove the chickens from the oven and let rest for a few minutes before carving.

To prepare the fennel, heat a sauté pan coated with nonstick cooking spray. Add the garlic and onions and sauté over medium-high heat for 2 to 3 minutes. Add the fennel and sauté for 2 or 3 minutes longer, being careful not to let it burn. Add the stock, vinegar, sugar, and white pepper, reduce the heat to medium-low, and simmer for 15 minutes. Drain most of the liquid from the pan, leaving about 1 tablespoon. Stir in the tomato and parsley and sauté for 2 minutes. Keep warm.

While the fennel is cooking, prepare the couscous. Heat a saucepan coated with nonstick cooking spray, and add the garlic and onions. Sauté over medium heat for 1 minute. Add the mushrooms and sauté for 3 to 5 minutes longer, until the mushrooms have released most of their liquid. Add the stock, thyme, parsley, and dill, increase to medium-high, and simmer for 5 minutes. Stir in the couscous, remove the pan from the heat, and let stand for 5 minutes. Fluff with a fork before serving.

To serve, place a mound of the couscous at the top of each plate. Spoon the fennel in the center of each plate and arrange about 4 ounces of sliced chicken per serving so that it leans against the fennel.

NOTES: Free-range chickens are grain fed and allowed to roam freely instead of being penned up in a coop, which gives their meat a higher proportion of muscle, and therefore flavor, compared to commercial birds. They are also free of hormones and steroids that mass-produced chickens tend to contain. Free-range chickens are not necessarily lower in fat, however; fat content has more to do with the particular breed (and there are more than 30 breeds raised in the United States).

NUTRITIONAL
INFORMATION PER
SERVING

Total Calories: 429

Total Fat: 9 gm.

Saturated Fat: 3 gm.

Cholesterol: 96 mg.

Sodium: 154 mg.

Fiber Rating: 8 gm.

Creamy Lemon Yogurt Mousse

This refreshing dessert has proven popular on Mother's Day. Its creamy, mousselike texture makes it hard to believe it's not loaded with calories and fat. Although I had never tasted yogurt until about 10 years ago, these days, I use it all the time.

SERVES: 4

2 teaspoons unflavored gelatin

3 tablespoons cold water

1 cup freshly squeezed lemon juice

8 tablespoons (¹/₂ cup) sugar

¹/₂ teaspoon minced lemon zest

3 egg whites

2 cups plain nonfat yogurt

4 sprigs mint, for garnish

NUTRITIONAL INFORMATION PER SERVING

Total Calories: 183

Total Fat: 0.2 gm.

Saturated Fat: 0

Cholesterol: 2 mg.

Sodium: 130 mg.

Fiber Rating: 0

Combine the gelatin and water in a saucepan and let soften for 1 to 2 minutes. Turn the heat to low, and thoroughly dissolve the gelatin over low heat while stirring, for about 4 or 5 minutes. Stir in the lemon juice and 6 tablespoons of the sugar, adding it 2 tablespoons at a time until each addition dissolves. Stir in the lemon zest and remove the pan from the heat.

Beat the egg whites in a mixing bowl until soft peaks form. Add the remaining 2 tablespoons of sugar and continue beating until stiff peaks form. Set aside.

Fold the yogurt into the gelatin mixture until well blended. Fold the beaten egg whites into the yogurt mixture. Pour the mixture into individual serving bowls and refrigerate until firm. Garnish each serving with a mint sprig.

NOTE: This is an excellent example of the versatility and value of nonfat yogurt. For those concerned about the calories and fat coming from ingredients used in sauces, soups, and desserts, nonfat yogurt makes a great replacement for dairy products such as sour cream, half-and-half, cream, or heavy cream.

Roasted Baby New Potato Salad

SERVES: 4

Certain foods are an integral part of special occasion menus, such as turkey at Thanksgiving. A barbecue is the focal point of any authentic Independence Day celebration, and in my home state of Texas, you can't have a barbecue without a traditional potato salad. Here's a heart-healthy potato salad without mayonnaise, using the red new potatoes traditional in the South.

NUTRITIONAL
INFORMATION PER
SERVING

Total Calories: 175

Total Fat: 7 gm.

Saturated Fat: 1 gm.

Cholesterol: 0 mg.

Sodium: 8 mg.

Fiber Rating: 0.1 gm.

1 pound red new potatoes, cut in half

2 tablespoons olive oil

$^1/_2$ tablespoons minced shallots

$^1/_2$ teaspoon minced garlic

$^1/_4$ cup seeded and diced red and green bell peppers

$^1/_4$ teaspoon pure red chile powder

1 teaspoon chopped fresh rosemary

1 teaspoon chopped fresh tarragon

$^1/_2$ tablespoon freshly squeezed lemon juice

$^1/_2$ tablespoon chopped fresh parsley

Freshly ground black pepper to taste

Preheat the oven to 400°.

Place the potatoes in a large nonstick baking dish and toss with the olive oil. Roast in the oven for 20 minutes, shaking the pan after about 10 minutes. Remove the pan from the oven and stir in the shallots, garlic, bell peppers, and chile powder. Return the pan to the oven and continue roasting for 15 minutes, or until the potatoes are soft. Remove the pan from the oven and transfer the potato mixture to a large mixing bowl.

Add the rosemary, tarragon, lemon juice, parsley, and black pepper and toss together. Serve at room temperature.

❧

NOTES: Like olive oil, mayonnaise contains fat, but it has more saturated fat. In addition, you need to use a lot more mayo than oil when making a potato salad, further increasing the total amount of fat consumed.

English Cucumber and Red Onion Slaw

Coleslaw is another Fourth of July tradition. This is a delicious, colorful version with a different twist. Instead of the usual cabbage, we use cooling cucumber. I prefer the long, thin English or hothouse variety in this recipe because it is less seedy and watery than regular cucumber. (If English cucumbers are unavailable, use regular cucumbers, but seed as well as peel them.) Because the mild rice wine vinegar has such low acidity, it is unnecessary to use any oil to cut it.

SERVES: 4

½ cup julienned red onions

1 English cucumber (about 12 ounces), peeled and julienned

½ tablespoon finely minced garlic

1 tablespoon minced fresh parsley

1 tablespoon chopped cilantro

3 tablespoons unseasoned rice wine vinegar

Pinch of freshly ground white pepper

Juice of ½ lime

NUTRITIONAL
INFORMATION PER
SERVING

Total Calories: 21

Total Fat: 0 gm.

Saturated Fat: 0 gm.

Cholesterol: 0 mg.

Sodium: 3 mg.

Fiber Rating: 1 gm.

Thoroughly combine all of the ingredients in a mixing bowl. Refrigerate for at least 2 hours before serving to allow the slaw to chill and for the flavors to marry.

NOTE: This is just the recipe if you want a dish that's very low in calories and fat to balance out dishes with higher calorie and fat contents.

Barbecued Spice-Rubbed Chicken with Chickeria Barbecue Sauce

SERVES: 4

The spice rub really gives the chicken some zip, and the barbecue sauce complements the rub perfectly. It's named "chickeria" after one of the upscale barbecue restaurants I owned in Dallas with my brother Hank in the early 1980s. The barbecue sauce attracted the attention of food magazines, and it was written up more than once. Use free-range chicken, if available, and serve with the accompanying recipes or a simple side of rice and/or beans.

BARBECUE SPICE RUB

1 teaspoon freshly ground black pepper

$1/2$ teaspoon cayenne

2 teaspoons pure chile powder

$2 1/2$ teaspoons ground cumin

1 teaspoon ground dried oregano

2 teaspoons paprika

1 teaspoon freshly ground white pepper

3 teaspoons granulated garlic

2 teaspoons granulated onion

2 teaspoons light brown sugar

4 boneless, skinless chicken breasts, about 5 ounces each

CHICKERIA BARBECUE SAUCE

$1/2$ cup chile sauce

2 tablespoons prepared Dijon mustard

2 tablespoons sodium-free soy sauce

2 tablespoons Cajun-style hot pepper sauce (such as Pickapeppa or Tabasco)

3 tablespoons light brown sugar

Juice of $1/2$ freshly squeezed lemon

3 tablespoons minced onions

1 tablespoon minced garlic

1 teaspoon freshly ground white pepper

Prepare the grill. Thoroughly mix together all the spice rub ingredients in a mixing bowl and set aside.

Combine all the barbecue sauce ingredients in a saucepan and, stirring occasionally, cook over medium heat for 5 to 10 minutes, until the flavors are thoroughly blended.

Rub the chicken breasts thoroughly with the spice rub. Transfer to the hot grill and cook for 5 minutes. Turn the chicken breasts over and cook for 2 minutes longer. Brush the chicken with the barbecue sauce and continue grilling for 2 to 3 minutes, or until cooked through.

Remove the chicken from the grill and let sit for a few minutes before serving.

❧

NOTE: The nutritional analysis assumes about 2 tablespoons of sauce per serving.

NUTRITIONAL INFORMATION PER SERVING

Total Calories: 158

Total Fat: 6 gm.

Saturated Fat: 2 gm.

Cholesterol: 65 mg.

Sodium: 101 mg.

Fiber Rating: 0 gm.

Blackberry Shortcake with Minted Orange Chantilly and Cilantro Oil

SERVES: 4

There is no more typical dessert for the American summer than simple shortcake. This refreshing version emphasizes the subtle flavors of the biscuit and the berries by relying on mint and citrus rather than on salt, which is commonly used in breads and cakes. A good biscuit dough should be sticky after mixing. The first reaction is to add more flour to firm it up. Instead, chill the dough until it firms up and can be handled. You can use the same amount of other types of berries, such as strawberries or raspberries, if blackberries are unavailable.

SHORTCAKE

$^3/_4$ cup all-purpose flour

2 tablespoons sugar

1 teaspoon baking powder

$^1/_4$ teaspoon ground allspice

2 tablespoons fat-free vegetable oil spread

$^1/_4$ cup nonfat milk

2 tablespoons egg substitute (such as Eggbeaters)

$^1/_4$ teaspoon pure vanilla extract

BERRY TOPPING

$1^1/_2$ pints fresh blackberries

1 tablespoon honey

2 tablespoons citrus-flavored vodka

Juice of $^1/_2$ freshly squeezed lime

CILANTRO OIL

$^1/_3$ cup olive oil

1 teaspoon honey

$^1/_4$ cup loosely packed cilantro

Pinch of salt

MINTED ORANGE CHANTILLY

$^1/_2$ cup nonfat milk

Minced zest of $^1/_4$ orange

$^1/_2$ tablespoon chopped fresh mint

1 package dried nonfat whipped topping mix (such as Rich's), or 3 tablespoons Cool Whip

Preheat the oven to 400°.

To prepare the shortcake, mix together the flour, sugar, baking powder, and allspice in a mixing bowl. Mix in the vegetable oil spread and set aside.

In a separate bowl, thoroughly combine the milk, egg substitute, and vanilla. Stir this mixture into the flour mixture until thoroughly combined; the dough will be very sticky. Cover and refrigerate or freeze the dough for at least 20 to 30 minutes, until firm enough to handle. Divide the dough into 4 equal portions and place on a baking sheet coated with nonstick cooking spray. Bake in the oven for 20 minutes, until golden brown. Remove the short-cakes from the oven and place on a wire rack to cool.

Meanwhile, to prepare the berry topping, combine the blackberries, honey, vodka, and lime in a small bowl and marinate for 1 hour.

To prepare the cilantro oil, place the ingredients in a blender and purée until emulsified. Set aside.

To prepare the chantilly, place the milk, orange zest, and mint in a small saucepan and bring just to a boil. Remove from the heat and let infuse for 10 minutes. Strain the mixture into a mixing bowl and refrigerate until cool. Add the whipped topping mix to the mixing bowl and beat until stiff. Set aside.

To assemble the dessert, cut each shortcake in half crosswise and place the bottoms on serving plates. Spoon the berry mixture on each shortcake bottom and top with the chantilly. Place the top half of the shortcake over the chantilly and drizzle each serving with 2 teaspoons of the cilantro oil.

NOTES: Dried nonfat topping mix is commonly available in the baking section of any large supermarket.

You can use the cilantro oil with fruit salads or any dessert with a high acid content; it cuts the sourness and acidity.

NUTRITIONAL INFORMATION PER SERVING

Total Calories: 291

Total Fat: 9 gm.

Saturated Fat: 2 gm.

Cholesterol: 2 mg.

Sodium: 187 mg.

Fiber Rating: 7 gm.

Three-Fish Chowder

A Christmas Eve tradition unique to Philadelphia is the Feast of the Seven Fishes, a local Catholic tradition celebrated by the Italian American community. The Philadelphia Inquirer *recently reported that the exact origins and significance of the feast are very sketchy, but it relates to the impending birth of Jesus. The exact nature of the feast varies from family to family; some use a different type of fish in each of seven courses, while others combine all seven fishes in one dish or course. This makes Christmas Eve a big day for the fish stores in town, especially in predominantly Italian neighborhoods like South Philly. This tradition gave me the idea for this chowder. It's a delicious, warming dish that's ideal for the holiday season. There's no need to go to the lengths of using seven types of fish, however, the more distinct the varieties you use, the more interesting the chowder becomes. The fish I use in this recipe have different textures, colors, and flavors. You can substitute the individual varieties of fish, but keep this principle in mind.*

SERVES: 4

5 ounces fresh swordfish, cut into 1-inch cubes

5 ounces fresh red snapper, cut into 1-inch cubes

5 ounces fresh salmon, cut into 1-inch cubes

2 teaspoons tomato paste

$1/3$ cup minced onions

1 teaspoon minced garlic

1 cup fennel bulb cut into 1-inch dice

3 cups Low-Sodium Fish Stock (page 229) or low-sodium clam juice

1 cup peeled baking or other potatoes, cut into 1-inch dice

2 tomatoes, cored and cut into 1-inch dice

2 teaspoons chopped fresh thyme

2 bay leaves

Pinch of freshly ground black pepper

Pinch of freshly ground white pepper

4 sprigs thyme, for garnish

NUTRITIONAL
INFORMATION PER
SERVING

Total Calories: 183

Total Fat: 5 gm.

Saturated Fat: 1 gm.

Cholesterol: 46 mg.

Sodium: 125 mg.

Fiber Rating: 2 gm

Cover the fish cubes with nonstick cooking spray on all sides. Heat a saucepan coated with nonstick cooking spray, add the fish, and sear on all sides over medium heat until brown. Remove the fish from the pan and set aside.

Add the tomato paste to the pan and stir with a wooden spoon for 2 to 3 minutes. Add the onions, garlic, and fennel, and cook for 1 minute, stirring constantly. Add the stock and bring the mixture to a simmer. Add the potatoes, tomatoes, thyme, and bay leaves, and simmer for about 20 minutes. Stir in the black and white pepper and continue cooking until the potatoes are tender. Stir in the seared fish and heat through.

To serve, ladle the chowder into soup bowls and garnish with the thyme sprigs.

NOTES: The American Heart Association and other agencies concerned with the prevention of heart disease encourage you to have at least 7 ounces of fish per week to provide a source of omega-3 fatty acids, which help prevent unwanted blood clotting. This recipe is a great way to add fish to your diet! Interestingly, saltwater fish do not contain more sodium than freshwater fish.

Haricots Verts and Balsamic-Glazed Salad

The seasonal colors of this dish—the green of the beans and bell pepper, the red of the onions and red bell pepper, and the orange carrot— give this salad a festive touch. This makes a healthy side-dish for the Thanksgiving or Christmas table.

SERVES: 4

GLAZE

$^3/_4$ cup balsamic vinegar

1 teaspoon minced garlic

$^1/_4$ cup Low-Sodium Chicken Stock (page 225)

1 teaspoon sugar

2 tablespoons minced fresh flat-leaf parsley

SALAD

3 cups haricots verts, trimmed to 2 inches long

$^1/_2$ cup grated carrots

1 cup thinly sliced red onions

$^1/_2$ cup seeded and julienned red bell pepper

$^1/_2$ cup seeded and julienned green bell pepper

$^1/_2$ cup sliced scallions

NUTRITIONAL INFORMATION PER SERVING

Total Calories: 109

Total Fat: 0.4 gm.

Saturated Fat: 0 gm.

Cholesterol: 0 mg.

Sodium: 17 mg.

Fiber Rating: 3 gm.

Combine all of the glaze ingredients in a saucepan and bring to a boil. Reduce the liquid by about half to three-quarters, until thickened and syrupy. Remove the glaze from the heat, stir in the parsley, and set aside.

To prepare the salad, bring a saucepan of lightly salted water to a boil. Add the beans and blanch for 4 to 5 minutes, until tender. Drain the beans and transfer immediately to an ice water bath. When cool, drain and transfer to a large mixing bowl. Add the carrots, onions, red and green bell peppers, and scallions. Add the glaze and toss together to coat evenly.

Herb-Rubbed Holiday Turkey with Creamy Polenta and Steamed Asparagus

SERVES: 4

*T*urkey is as traditional as it gets for Thanksgiving and the holiday season. The bird is native to the Americas—in fact, Benjamin Franklin proposed that the turkey become the national emblem of the United States rather than the belligerent eagle. Placing the herbs under the skin of the turkey protects them from burning up, and they give the breast meat an intense, infused flavor.

TURKEY

1 turkey (about 12 pounds)

2 tablespoons chopped fresh thyme leaves (stems reserved)

2 tablespoons chopped fresh rosemary needles (stems reserved)

2 tablespoons chopped fresh sage leaves (stems reserved)

2 tablespoons minced garlic

2 tablespoons minced shallots

Freshly ground black pepper to taste

3 lemons, cut in half

ASPARAGUS

20 asparagus spears

Pinch of salt

Freshly ground white pepper to taste

Juice of $1/2$ freshly squeezed lemon

CREAMY POLENTA

$1/4$ cup finely diced onions

1 tablespoon minced garlic

$1/4$ cup seeded and finely diced red bell pepper

$1/4$ cup seeded and finely diced green bell pepper

3 cups Low-Sodium Chicken Stock (page 225)

1 cup cornmeal

$1/4$ cup minced fresh parsley

$1/4$ cup fresh basil chiffonade

Freshly ground white pepper to taste

Preheat the oven to 350°.

To prepare the turkey, gently pull the skin away from the meat at the neck end by sliding your fingers under the skin as far as possible. In a mixing bowl, combine the thyme, rosemary, sage, garlic, shallots, and pepper. Rub this mixture onto the turkey meat in the pocket you have made underneath the skin. Squeeze the juice of 1 lemon over the whole turkey, and place the remaining 2 lemons in the cavity together with the reserved herb stems.

Place the turkey in a roasting pan and transfer to the oven. Roast for 3 hours, or until the internal temperature reaches 150° on a meat thermometer, or the juices run clear when the base of the leg is pierced by a sharp knife. Let the turkey rest for 15 to 20 minutes so the juices can settle before carving.

Meanwhile, to prepare the polenta, heat a saucepan coated with nonstick cooking spray. Add the onion, garlic, and bell peppers, and sauté over medium heat for about 2 minutes, until softened. Remove the pan from the heat and set aside.

Place the stock in a separate saucepan and bring to a boil. Slowly, but briskly, whisk in the cornmeal. Reduce the heat, stirring constantly, cook the mixture for about 15 minutes, until creamy. Stir in the onion mixture, the parsley, basil, and white pepper, and keep warm.

To prepare the asparagus, bring a large saucepan of water fitted with a steamer basket to a boil. Bend the asparagus spears in half until they break. Discard the stalk halves and place the tip halves in the steamer basket. Steam for about 5 minutes or until tender, depending on their thickness. Remove the asparagus from the basket and transfer to an ice water bath. When cool, drain thoroughly and place in a bowl. Season with the salt, white pepper, and lemon juice, and set aside.

To serve, place a mound of the polenta in the center of each serving plate and fan about 4 ounces of the turkey breast slices around the polenta, leaning against it. Garnish each serving with 5 asparagus spears, and serve immediately.

NUTRITIONAL INFORMATION PER SERVING
Total Calories: 319
Total Fat: 5 gm.
Saturated Fat: 1 gm.
Cholesterol: 79 mg.
Sodium: 152 mg.
Fiber Rating: 6 gm.

Red Yam Corn Cake with Pumpkin Mousse

SERVES: 6

Most people think yams are the same thing as sweet potatoes (the words are used interchangeably in many regions), but in fact, even though they look and taste similar, they are two different species. Yams are native to Africa; sweet potatoes to the New World. Yams were brought to the West Indies by African slaves, and they were also taken by explorers eastward, so they are widely consumed in Asia. Yams are sweeter and have a higher water content than sweet potatoes. Having made these distinctions, you may by all means substitute the sweet potato for the yam. If you wish, you may serve the pumpkin mousse on its own, perhaps accompanied by cookies.

CAKE

$^1/_2$ cup granulated sugar

2 egg whites

$^1/_2$ cup yam purée (about 1 medium yam)

$1^1/_2$ tablespoons cornmeal

$^1/_2$ cup all-purpose flour

$^1/_4$ cup corn oil

$^1/_2$ teaspoon ground ginger

$^1/_4$ teaspoon ground cardamom

$^1/_8$ teaspoon ground mace

PUMPKIN MOUSSE

$^2/_3$ cup pumpkin purée

2 tablespoons brown sugar

$^1/_4$ teaspoon ground cinnamon

2 teaspoons cold water

$^1/_2$ teaspoon powdered gelatin

3 egg whites

ORANGE CARAMEL

$^3/_4$ cup granulated sugar

$^1/_2$ cup freshly squeezed orange juice

Preheat the oven to 350°.

To prepare the cake, place the sugar, egg whites, yam purée, and cornmeal in a mixing bowl. Using a heavy duty electric mixer on medium speed, thoroughly mix together until smooth.

In a separate mixing bowl, combine the flour and baking powder. Stir in the yam mixture and the corn oil, alternating each as you mix. Fold in the spices and adjust the seasonings as desired. Pour the batter into 6 muffin cups that have been coated with nonstick cooking spray. Bake in the oven for about 20 minutes, until a toothpick inserted comes out clean. Remove from the oven and let cool before unmolding.

To prepare the mousse, thoroughly mix together the pumpkin purée, brown sugar, and cinnamon in a mixing bowl. Set aside. Place the cold water in the top of a double boiler. Sprinkle the gelatin over the water and heat over simmering water, stirring constantly until the gelatin is dissolved.

With a heavy duty electric mixer on high speed, beat the egg whites in a mixing bowl until firm peaks form. Fold into the pumpkin mixture, and then fold in the gelatin mixture. Refrigerate until ready to use.

To prepare the orange caramel, slowly heat the sugar in a nonstick sauté pan over medium heat. When it begins to caramelize, add the orange juice in small increments, stirring after each addition. Cook until no lumps remain.

Cut each cake across in half, and place a small scoop of the chilled mousse between the layers. Transfer to serving plates and drizzle the orange caramel over the cake. Add a small dollop of nondairy topping, if desired.

NOTE: If you are using canned pumpkin purée, check the label. If sugar or sweetener has already been added, reduce the amount of sugar in the mousse recipe by half, or to taste.

NUTRITIONAL INFORMATION PER SERVING

Total Calories: 334

Total Fat: 9 gm.

Saturated Fat: 1 gm.

Cholesterol: 0

Sodium: 59 mg.

Fiber Rating: 1 gm.

Basic Recipes and Techniques

Low-Sodium Chicken Stock

T his recipe contains approximately 8 milligrams of sodium per cup, compared to the 1,500 milligrams per cup in some canned stocks. The bouquet garni can be made with dried herbs if fresh herbs are unavailable. In that case, simpy place $^1/_4$ teaspoon each of dried parsley, thyme, and basil together with $^1/_8$ teaspoon each of dried marjoram and tarragon in a double layer of cheesecloth, and tie securely.

YIELD: 1 TO
1 $^1/_2$ QUARTS

3 quarts cold water

3 pounds chicken bones (for turkey stock, substitute turkey bones)

2 large onions, chopped

1 carrot, sliced

2 celery stalks, sliced

BOUQUET GARNI:

1 sprig parsley

1 sprig thyme

1 sprig basil

1 sprig marjoram

1 sprig tarragon

1 bay leaf

2 cloves garlic, sliced (optional)

1 celery stalk, with leaves

Place the water, chicken bones, onions, carrot, and celery in a stockpot or large saucepan and bring to a boil.

To prepare the bouquet garni, stack the herbs and garlic on top of the celery stalk and tie securely. Add to the pan. Reduce the heat to low, cover partially, and simmer for about 5 hours, occasionally skimming off any fat or impurities. Add water as needed to keep the ingredients just covered.

Strain the stock into a large bowl and let stand for 15 minutes. Carefully skim the fat and then strain the stock through cheesecloth into a second bowl. Refrigerate until the fat congeals on the surface, then skim off the fat. Cover and store in the refrigerator for up to 1 week, or freeze for up to 3 months.

Low-Sodium Beef Stock

YIELD: 2
QUARTS

Many people think that making beef stock is too difficult to do at home, but it is surprisingly easy and not at all labor-intensive. Make more than you need for any particular recipe and refrigerate or freeze the rest. Ask your butcher to cut the beef bones into 3- or 4-inch pieces so they are easier to roast. If you find that the finished stock is not as flavorful as you like, bring it to a boil, uncovered, and reduce until the flavor intensifies. This technique may be used for the other stocks as well.

4 pounds beef bones

1 pound beef chuck, cut into 2-inch cubes

3 quarts cold water

1 onion, chopped

2 carrots, sliced

3 celery stalks, sliced

2 cloves garlic, crushed

1 bay leaf

1 sprig thyme, or $1/4$ teaspoon dried thyme

5 peppercorns, crushed

$1/4$ cup unsalted tomato paste, or 2 tomatoes, chopped

$1/2$ cup white wine

Preheat the oven to 350°.

Wash the beef bones in cold water and place in a shallow roasting pan in a single layer. Roast in the oven for 30 to 40 minutes, stirring occasionally. Transfer the bones to a stockpot and drain off the fat.

Pour 2 to 3 cups of the cold water into the roasting pan and deglaze over medium heat. Add this liquid to the stockpot with the bones. Add the remaining water to the stockpot and bring to a simmer.

Spray a nonstick sauté pan with a light coating of nonstick cooking spray and sauté the onion, carrots, celery, and garlic for 6 to 8 minutes over medium heat, until evenly browned. Drain the vegetables well and add to the stockpot with the bay leaf, thyme, peppercorns, tomato paste, and wine. Return the stock to a simmer and cook, uncovered, for 6 to 8 hours, occasionally skimming any fat or impurities that rise to the surface. Add water as needed to keep the ingredients just covered.

Strain the stock into a large bowl and let stand for 15 minutes. Carefully skim the fat and then strain the stock through cheesecloth into a second bowl. Refrigerate until the fat congeals on the surface, then skim off the fat. Cover and store in the refrigerator for 3 or 4 days, or freeze for up to 3 months.

VARIATION: For low-sodium veal stock use the beef stock recipe, but substitute veal bones and veal chuck for the beef. Add 1 or 2 oregano sprigs if desired.

Low-Sodium Lamb Stock

For an especially flavorful stock, use a mixture of lamb bones, trimmings, and lamb meat rather than just trimmings.

YIELD: 1 1/2 QUARTS

2 pounds lamb trimmings and additional meat as necessary

3 quarts cold water

1 onion, chopped

1 small carrot, sliced

2 cloves garlic, crushed

2 sprigs parsley

1 sprig rosemary

3 peppercorns, crushed

Preheat the oven to 350°.

Place the lamb trimmings in a shallow roasting pan in a single layer. Roast in the oven for 30 minutes, until browned, and drain off the fat.

Bring the cold water to a boil in a stockpot and add the roasted lamb trimmings, onion, carrot, garlic, parsley, rosemary, and peppercorns. Reduce the heat to medium and simmer, uncovered, for 5 to 6 hours, occasionally skimming any fat or impurities that rise to the surface. Add water as needed to keep the ingredients just covered.

Strain the stock into a large bowl and let stand for 15 minutes. Carefully skim the fat and then strain the stock through cheesecloth into a second bowl. Refrigerate until the fat congeals on the surface; then skim off the fat. Cover and store in the refrigerator for 3 to 4 days, or freeze for up to 3 months.

Low-Sodium Fish Stock

Preferably use the bones of firmly-textured white fish and avoid those of oily fish such as salmon as they don't make a great stock. Use the head and tail of filleted whole fish, but do not use the gills, which add a bitter flavor. It's important you start with cold water so the flavors will emerge gradually and not be sealed in immediately.

YIELD: 2 QUARTS

5 pounds fish bones (sole, halibut, sea bass, or other white-fleshed fish)

3 quarts cold water

1 small onion, chopped

$^1/_2$ carrot, sliced

1 celery stalk, sliced

1 cup mushroom stems or slices

1 sprig fennel

1 sprig thyme

3 sprigs parsley

1 bay leaf

4 peppercorns, crushed

Wash the bones in cold water and place in a stockpot with all of the ingredients. Bring to a simmer, skimming and discarding any foam or impurities that rise to the surface. Continue to simmer for 45 minutes. Add water as needed to keep all the ingredients just covered.

Strain the stock into a large bowl and let stand for 15 minutes. Carefully skim any foam or impurities from the surface. Cover and store in the refrigerator for up to 3 days, or freeze for up to 3 months.

Low-Sodium Vegetable Stock

Use this stock whenever you want a substitute for one of the meat-based stocks. It will keep for up to one week in the refrigerator, or you can freeze it for up to 3 months.

YIELD: 2
QUARTS

3 quarts cold water

1 onion, chopped

1 leek, sliced

2 carrots, sliced

2 celery stalks, sliced

1 tomato, diced

1 cup sliced mushrooms (optional)

3 cloves garlic, chopped

2 bay leaves

2 sprigs thyme

2 sprigs parsley

2 sprigs cilantro

5 black peppercorns, crushed

Place all of the ingredients in a large stockpot and bring to a boil. Reduce the heat to low, cover partially, and simmer for 30 minutes. Remove from the heat, cover, and let stand for 15 minutes. Strain and discard the solids. Use as needed, or store for later use.

Roasting Bell Peppers and Chiles

This technique gives bell peppers and fresh chiles a roasted flavor and brings out their full sweetness. It also makes them much easier to peel.

Preheat the broiler or prepare the grill. Spray or brush each pepper or chile lightly with olive oil. Place under the broiler or on the grill and turn frequently with tongs until the skin is blackened on all sides. Take care not to burn the flesh. When the peppers are charred, transfer to a bowl, cover the bowl with plastic wrap, and let cool for 10 minutes. Remove the plastic wrap and peel the blackened skin with the tip of a sharp knife. Remove the stems, cut the peppers or chiles open lengthwise, and remove the seeds, core, and pale internal ribs. Chop, dice, or slice, and set aside until ready to use.

Toasting Pumpkin Seeds

This technique brings out a roastiness and intensifies the rich flavor of the pumpkin seeds. Place the seeds in a single layer in a hot, dry skillet over medium-high heat for 2 to 3 minutes, stirring with a wooden spoon. The seeds will pop and brown slightly. Take care not to burn the seeds.

This technique can be used with other seeds, as well as with nuts, dried herbs, and spices. Smaller seeds and herbs and spices will toast more quickly (1 to 2 minutes), and should be toasted over medium heat, while most nuts will take longer (up to 5 to 7 minutes). These ingredients are toasted when they brown slightly and become aromatic.

Index